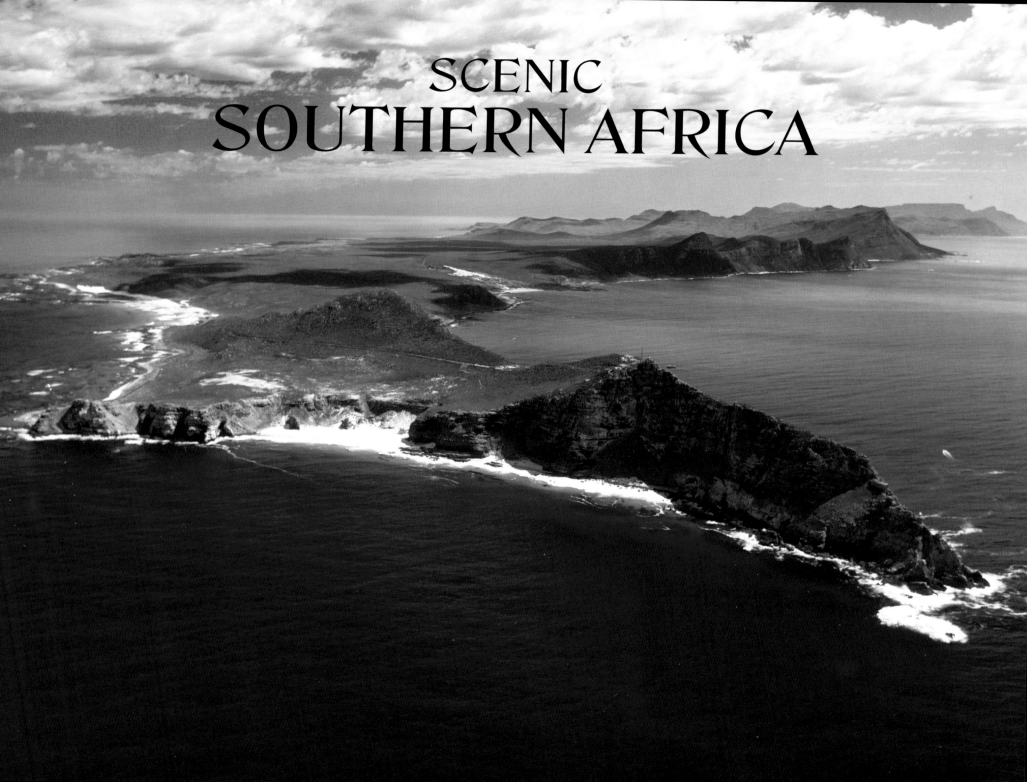

SCENIC
SOUTHERN AFRICA

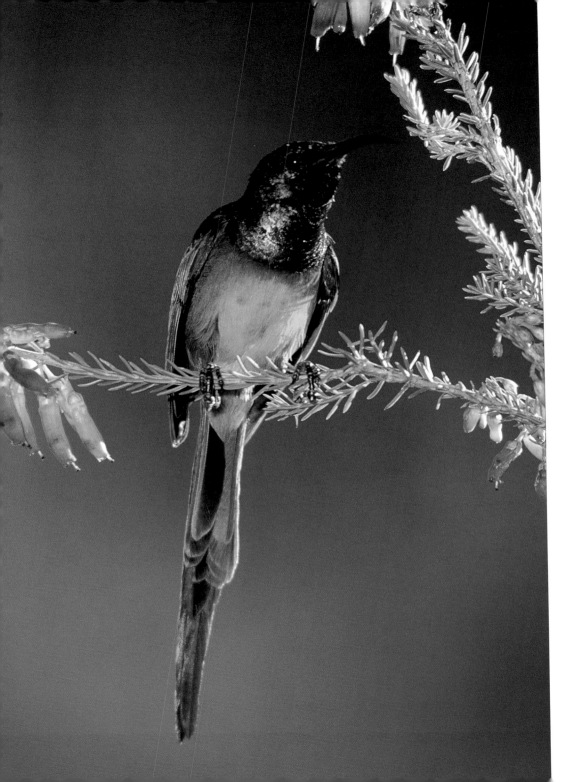

SUNBIRD
PUBLISHERS

First Published 2005
2 4 6 8 10 9 7 5 3 1

Sunbird Publishers (Pty) Ltd
P O Box 6836, Roggebaai, 8012 Cape Town, South Africa

www.sunbirdpublishers.co.za

Registration number: 4850177827

Publisher Natanya Mulholland
Editor Annlerie van Rooyen
Designer Mandy McKay
Production Manager Andrew de Kock

Reproduction by Unifoto (Pty) Ltd, Cape Town
Printed and bound by Tien Wah Press (Pte) Ltd, Singapore

ISBN 1 919 93819 2

FLY WITH THE SUNBIRDS
Dedicated to the memory of Brenda Brickman and Dick Wilkins, whose
friendship, wisdom and courage continue to inspire all those with whom
they worked over the years and with whom they shared a special vision.
Their passion for books and for life itself will remain with us forever.

TITLE PAGE *As part of the greater Table Mountain National Park, Cape Point forms the heart*
of the Cape of Good Hope Nature Reserve on the Cape Peninsula.
LEFT AND OPPOSITE *Sunbirds are fairly common in the northern, eastern and southwestern*
parts of the country, the males boasting especially brilliant plumage. The colourful attire of,
for example, the orangebreasted (left) and lesser doublecollared sunbirds (opposite) make them
among the most recognisable of local species.

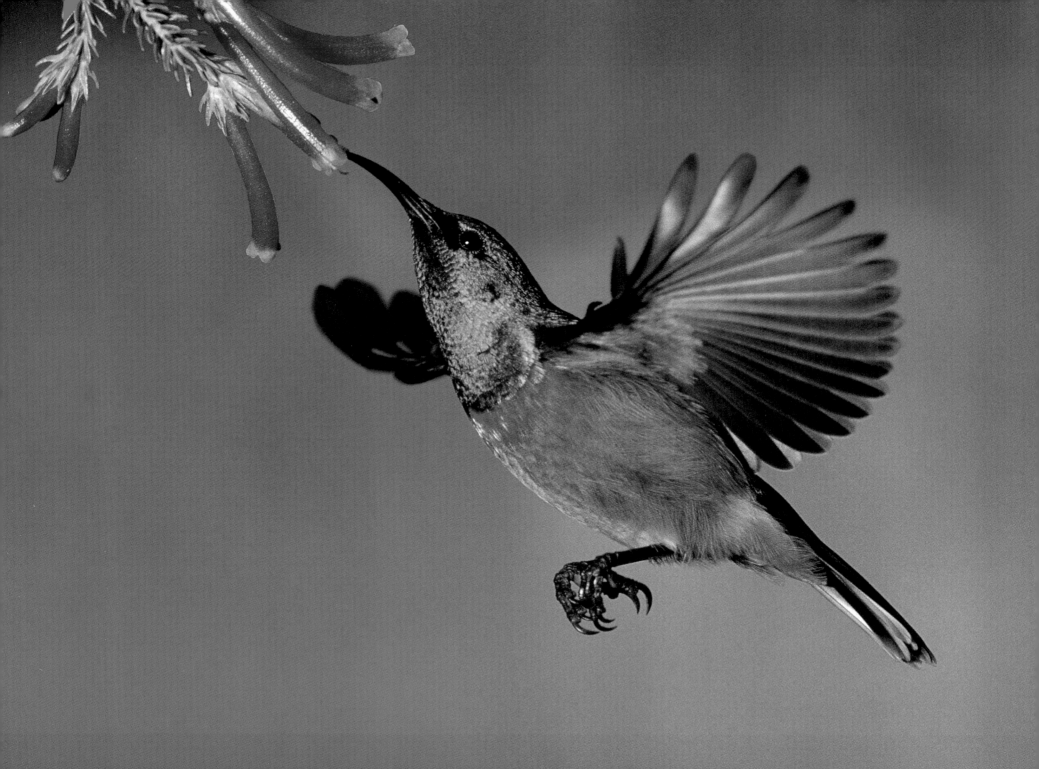

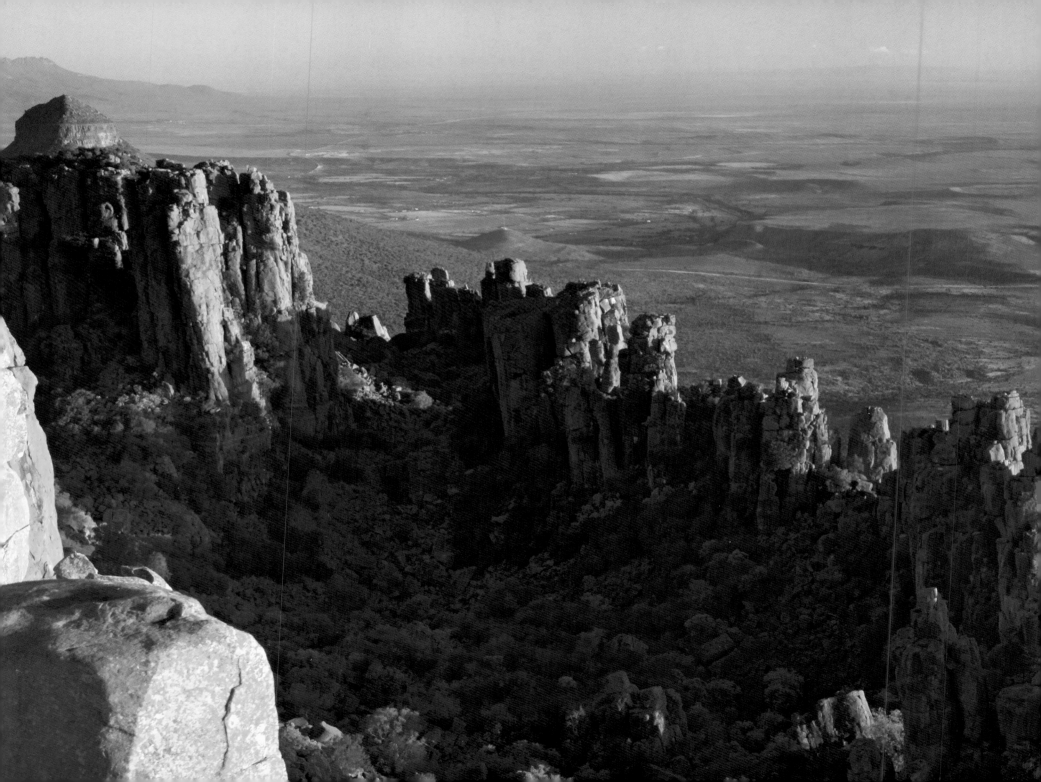

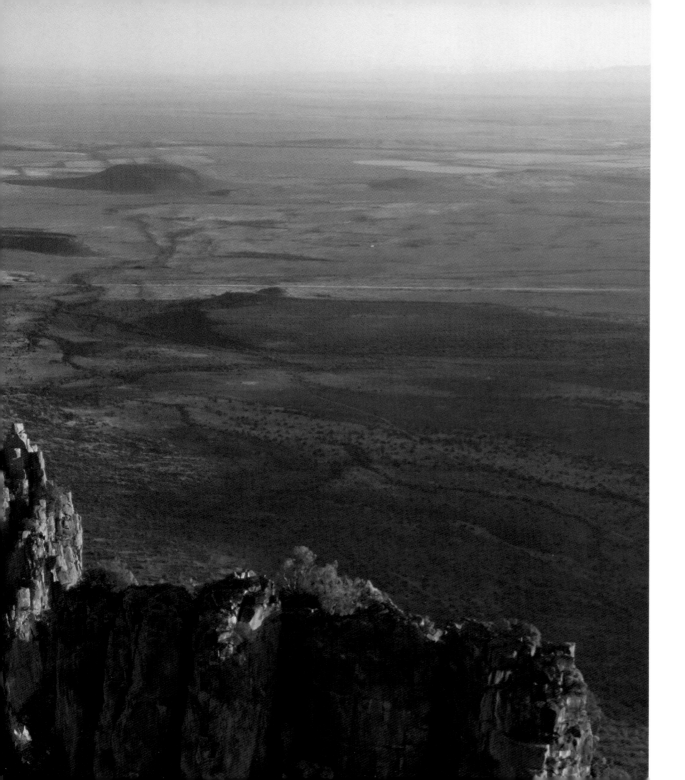

Contents

LEFT *Despite the sombre and subdued colours that epitomise the moonscape of the Valley of Desolation, its towering rock pillars offer spectacular views of the Great Karoo.*

Introducing Southern Africa

The romantic notion of pastoralist Africa is one that wistfully invokes visions of blazing sunsets, lone acacia trees silhouetted by a silver moon and dusty plains extending beyond never-ending horizons. These are the images most visitors to Africa expect to encounter on their travels. For Africans, however, these are the scenes they wake up to every day – and nowhere is this more true than in southern Africa, where all the faces of this unpredictable continent gather on but a small portion of an otherwise vast landmass. The wilds of southern Africa comprise some of the most unspoilt and undeveloped stretches on Earth and the countries that make up this distinct geographical region – South Africa, Namibia,

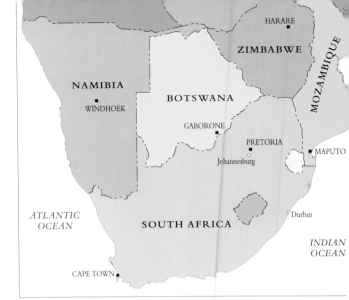

Mozambique, Botswana and Zimbabwe – cover a wilderness of some 3 820 000 square kilometres (1 500 000 square miles). Encompassing these vast expanses are regions of enormous biodiversity that range from pristine coastal plain and rocky mountain passes to thickly treed woodland and endless savannas. Here, too, scattered across the extraordinarily diverse landscape are pockets of humanity

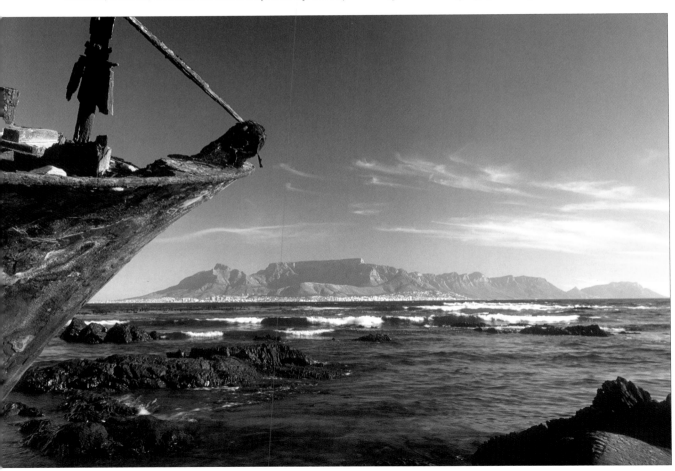

ABOVE While southern Africa may be a vast place with many different and often contrasting faces, it is the face of Cape Town's Table Mountain that is its most recognisable landmark.

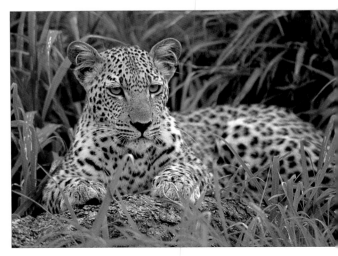

ABOVE The region has abundant wildlife, and yet it is the Big Five – including the leopard – that feature highest on the game-viewer's list.

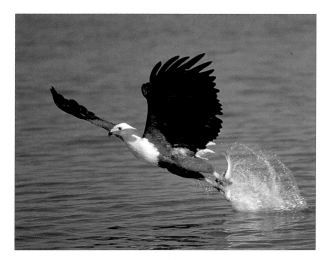

ABOVE *Because southern Africa's landscapes are so different, its birdlife is equally diverse – the African fish eagle's call is indicative.*

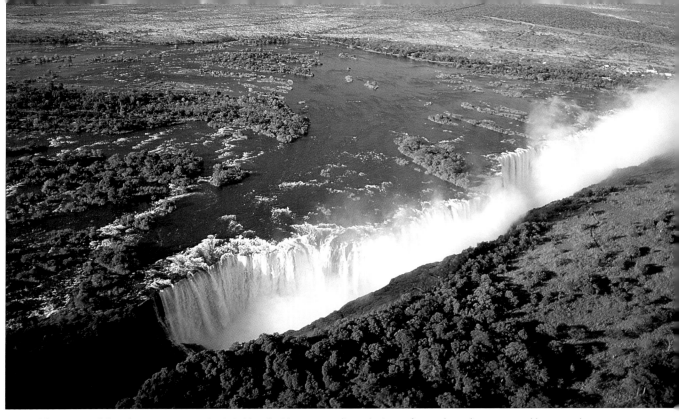

ABOVE *The vastness of the subcontinent means that it is blessed with an extraordinary heritage of natural wonders, most notable among these the great Victoria Falls on the Zambezi River between Zimbabwe and Zambia.*

occupying anything from small rural villages to sprawling urban settlements that contribute not a little to the ever-changing face of not only southern Africa, but also the continent as a whole.

The subcontinent remains one of Africa's great draw-cards – it is home to vast numbers of endemic wildlife, the setting of some of the continent's most inspiring vistas and proud host to some of Africa's greatest game reserves and national parks. With the growing demands of Africa's human population of approximately 800 million, it is a remarkable achievement, then, that so much remains relatively untouched by human influence. The potential for a burgeoning tourism, ecotourism and hospitality industry – and the great wealth that this may mean to a largely impoverished society – offers enormous scope for developing the regional economy. And herein lies southern Africa's most promising contribution.

While the subcontinent's gazetted parks, reserves, conservation lands and wildlife sanctuaries may vary considerably in both size and stature, they remain the most

sought-after adventure and safari destinations in the world. Indeed, there is growing international interest in southern Africa's wild places, from the spring-flowering fields of South Africa's Namaqualand to the swamplands of Botswana's Okavango. The game-viewing and bird-watching are unparalleled, and the list of adventures and holiday opportunities seem endless as southern Africa welcomes more and more visitors to its natural splendour.

Considering the fact that Africa, as a whole, is blessed with great, open spaces, a vast, winding coastline and a remarkable number and diversity of wildlife, the conservation of this legacy is vital to the future of the continent. In this regard, the nations that make up southern Africa have taken the lead in one of the most inspiring

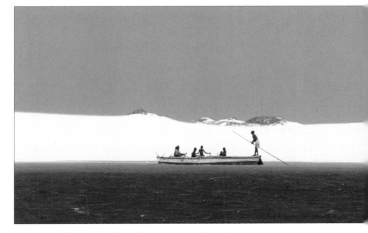

ABOVE *While small pockets of Mozambique have been given over to resorts, much of the country is unspoilt.*

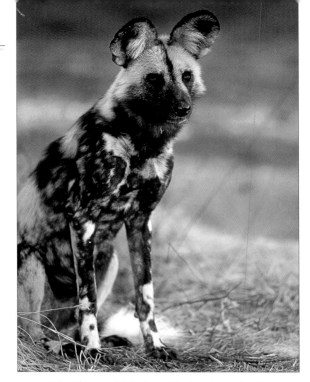

ABOVE *The African wild dog has suffered at the hands of hunters and poachers, with large numbers decimated.*

conservation efforts the world has seen – the establishment of transfrontier parks, international agreements between neighbouring countries on land that transcends national

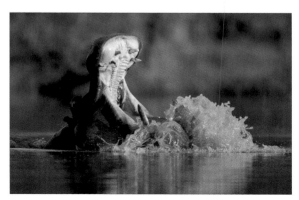

ABOVE *The Big Five attract the largest number of game-viewers but the hippo is one of Africa's largest mammals.*

boundaries. These collaborative trans-border programmes rely on the mutual cooperation of participating countries, thus ensuring not only the preservation of the land, its people and the wildlife of the specific areas covered by these parks, but also regional development that will go a long way in improving the standard of living of the communities that are directly involved in the ecotourism projects that grow from these agreements.

While the initial aim was to set up about six of these transfrontier parks, no fewer than 20 sites have already been earmarked as cross-border conservation areas – and the most ambitious and significant of these are to be found in southern Africa, the first to implement projects of this nature. The Kgalagadi Transfrontier Park between Botswana and South Africa was, in fact, the continent's first formal transnational reserve. It has since been emulated with, for example, the Gaza-Kruger-Gonarezhou Transfrontier Park crossing the political boundaries of South Africa, Mozambique and Zimbabwe, the Maloti-Drakensberg Transfrontier Park between South Africa and the kingdom of Lesotho and the

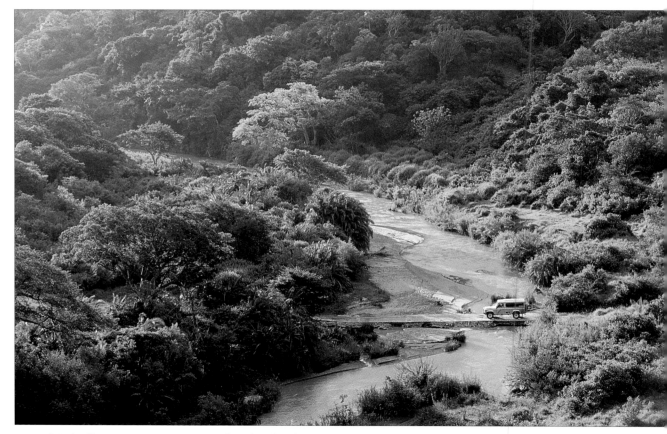

ABOVE *It is the all-important water sources in parks such as the Hluhluwe-Imfolozi National Park in KwaZulu-Natal which remain the centre of activity for both wildlife and visitors to South Africa's conservation areas.*

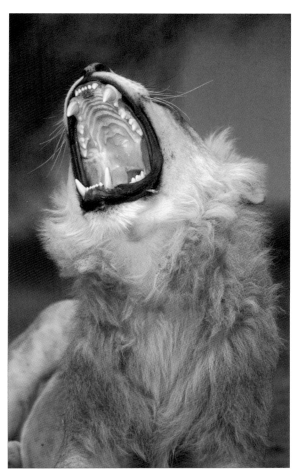

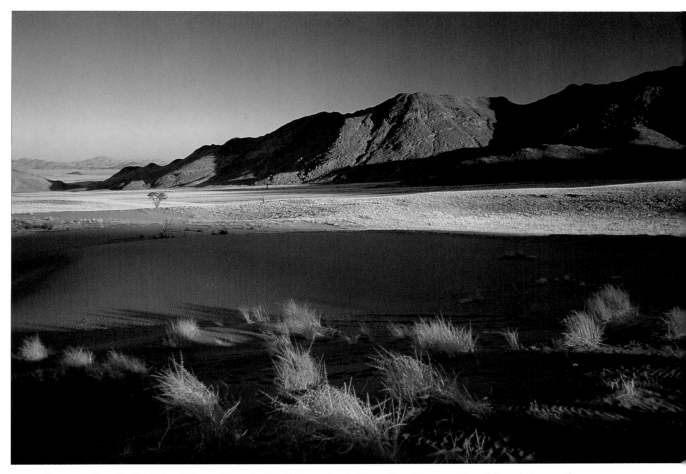

ABOVE   While plenty of mammals attract great numbers of game-viewers to the parks, it is the lion that remains the big attraction.

ABOVE   Reserves, such as the NamibRand Nature Reserve in Namibia, remain vital not only to the conservation of the region's unspoilt nature, but also to the tourism industry, which continues to play a pivotal role in the local economy.

Great Limpopo Transfrontier Park, some 100 000 square kilometres (40 000 square miles) spanning parts of Zimbabwe, Mozambique and South Africa.

Together, South Africa, Namibia, Botswana, Zimbabwe and Mozambique have managed – in spite of all the social and political issues that still pervade so much of the continent north of the Limpopo – to make the most of their spectacular scenery, the indigenous wildlife and the warm hospitality of their peoples. Balancing the demands of thriving – and growing – tourism industries with the requirements of an often precarious ecology remains the central issue for all these countries. The enormous range of their wild spaces and natural habitats, from coastal wetlands and bushveld landscape to mountains and even desert sands, means that there is an equally varied flora and fauna. Birds abound in every form, their mammals include the largest, the smallest and certainly in the case of the Big Five, for example, the most impressive. It is, however, perhaps the people more than all of this that make the nations of southern Africa such a fascinating microcosm of the rest of Africa. In every face, on every city street and in every dusty village are the real images of Africa at its finest and it is here, in southern Africa, that the world gets to experience the essence of the continent and, more significantly, the subcontinent.

South Africa

Centuries before European colonists laid claim to the riches of southern Africa, these lands were trammelled by the indigenous Khoisan, a wandering group who survived off what their environment could offer – fish and other seafoods from the waters of both the Atlantic and Indian oceans, antelope meat from the inland plains and a variety of small game that provided not only sustenance but also day-to-day necessities such as hides for clothing and animal fats for cooking purposes. The descendants of this remarkably innovative Stone Age community were the original settlers of what we today know as South Africa.

While the landscape may have changed since those early days and there is no longer the abundance of wildlife that once roamed this untamed wilderness, what remains is a world of equal beauty and equally breathtaking proportions.

South Africa, covering the southernmost reaches of the subcontinent, consists largely of wide open spaces ranging from white coastal stretches – including the picturesque Garden Route – to towering mountain vistas, arid desert to

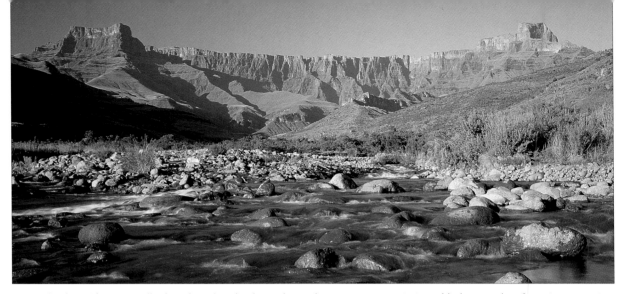

ABOVE *Southern Africa, especially along the rocky ridge that makes up the great escarpment, is rimmed by long stretches of towering mountain peaks, and nowhere is this more spectacular than in the Drakensberg's Amphitheatre.*

sparsely vegetated savanna and sweeping grasslands. In parts dry and desolate and in others abundantly green and fertile, the contrasting faces of South Africa have made it one of the continent's top wildlife and tourism destinations. Prime attractions include a diverse wildlife, one that is at its most impressive in the big-game regions of KwaZulu-Natal and Mpumalanga (most notably, the Kruger National Park), and an unrivalled natural heritage that covers not only the extraordinary landscape but also a rich tapestry of cultural influences. These have ensured that South Africa enjoys an international interest as a tourist destination, and it has developed into a prominent player in the sociopolitical and economic arena of the continent as a whole.

With a total land area of 1 221 040 square kilometres (471 443 square miles), South Africa boasts a remarkable 13 million hectares (32 million acres) of conservation land and protected areas officially recognised by the United Nations. Even though the majority of the individual sites are quite small – most covering less than 10 000 hectares (24 700 acres) – this nevertheless makes it one of Africa's most conservation-conscious nations. There are some 17 national parks and over

1 000 reserves as well as about 500 private game farms. These sanctuaries hold some of the most impressive conservation records in the world and some of the most significant – and comprehensive – wildlife management systems in Africa, lauded across the globe for the sound principles adopted in the utilisation of the country's wildlife resources. One of the priorities is protecting the Big Five (lion, leopard, buffalo, rhino and elephant) and whales, which are now part of what is commonly referred to as the Big Six – all of which are prime tourist attractions to South Africa's wildlife and coastal areas. Also receiving special attention from conservation authorities – and the all-important tourist market – is the country's indigenous vegetation, the most prominent being the magnificent floral display of Namaqualand and other significant ecotourist destinations.

In stark contrast to the sprawling urban settlements of, for example, Gauteng, the face of the country is generally wild and, in many parts, relatively empty of people. South Africa's nine provinces cover no fewer than seven vegetation biomes, including more than 15 protected wetland areas. Among other fiercely protected areas are a number of

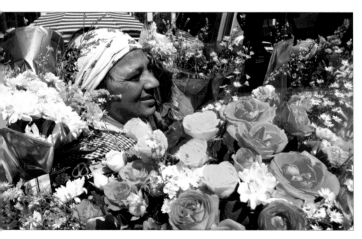

ABOVE *Beyond landscapes and wildlife, it is South Africa's people – here a Cape flower seller – who are a true reflection of the nation.*

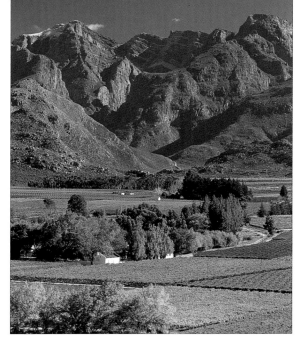

ABOVE The Cape hinterland, including the bountiful Hex River Valley, is an especially green and productive region.

exclusive World Heritage Sites, notably the Cradle of Humankind at the Sterkfontein Caves, Mapungubwe, the Drakensberg mountain range, the Greater St Lucia Wetland

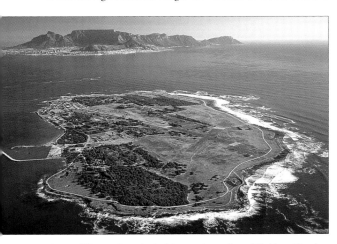

ABOVE The rough and wind-battered coastline of Robben Island made it an ideal place to which to banish prisoners of yesteryear.

Park, Table Mountain National Park and Robben Island. A few other such sites, equally significant as conservation areas, are currently under consideration for similar status.

At the last official count, South Africa's population stood at 42.4 million, with some 75 per cent comprising indigenous black groups, 14 per cent white, 9 per cent of mixed descent and 2 per cent Asian. When it comes to the country's urban centres, most of these population groups are well represented, but rural communities tend to consist largely of groups who have traditionally been resident in the area for centuries. Here, the rural people of South Africa have nurtured age-old customs and traditions, and continue to hone their skills as masterful craftsmen and -women. South Africa is, in fact, world renowned for the indigenous craftwork of its many peoples. From the intricate beadwork of the Zulu people and the ceramics and textiles of the Xhosa to the colours of Ndebele murals, the skills required offer a glimpse into centuries of a rich legacy. Traditional South African art – much like that of Zimbabwe, Botswana, Namibia and Mozambique – remains a sought-after commodity and, with the remarkable growth in the local hospitality industry, is now more readily available than ever before, with many skilled craftsfolk enthusiastically bartering the sale of their goods in both rural and urban areas.

South Africa's cities and large towns, on the other hand, combine traditional Africa with the modern conveniences of the developed world. It is here that grand old edifices dating from the colonial periods in local history stand amid blocks of high-rise offices. Lively market squares are linked by a network of wide avenues, dusty side streets and cobbled alleys, with the informal traders of today playing a vital role in the country's economic sector.

Both Johannesburg and Cape Town, the former the economic heart of the nation and the latter the Cannes of Africa, are considered sophisticated metropolitan centres that boast all the conveniences of any modern city. And much the same can be said for other prominent urban settlements, such as Pretoria/Tshwane, Durban, Pietermaritzburg, Kimberley, Bloemfontein and Port Elizabeth. By and large, South Africa's cities are a good mix of contemporary life and a gentler, laidback lifestyle: grand hotels, busy malls and massive entertainment complexes serve to complement the boundless reserves and parks that dot the countryside. But while urban South Africa is a world of extremes, large melting pots of cultural diversity and a mix of the ancient and the modern, for many Western travellers crossing the subcontinent they serve as little more than embarkation points for the untamed wilderness far beyond the urban limits. The jammed intersections, teeming thoroughfares and lively pedestrian traffic of the cities are a long way from South Africa's great legacy of mountain, bushveld, beach and grassy plain.

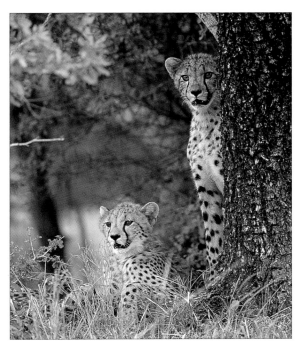

ABOVE While South Africa has many impressive reserves Kruger – home of the cheetah, among others – is by far the most popular.

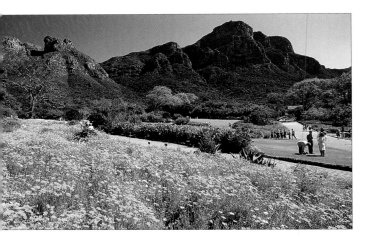

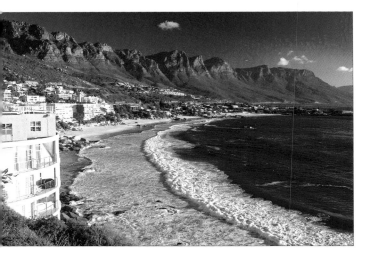

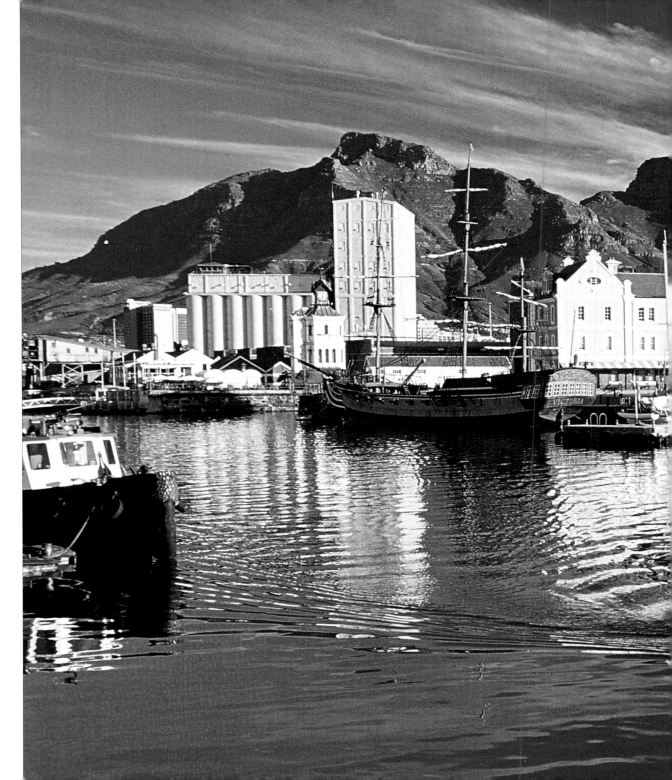

TOP The national botanical gardens at Kirstenbosch on the Cape Peninsula are recognised worldwide as the greatest treasure house of southern African flora.

ABOVE One of the principal drawcards to South Africa, and Cape Town especially, is the scenic beauty of its many beaches, including the ever-popular Clifton.

RIGHT Cape Town's Victoria & Alfred Waterfront is a lively, modern shopping and entertainment complex skirting the water's edge of spectacular Table Bay.

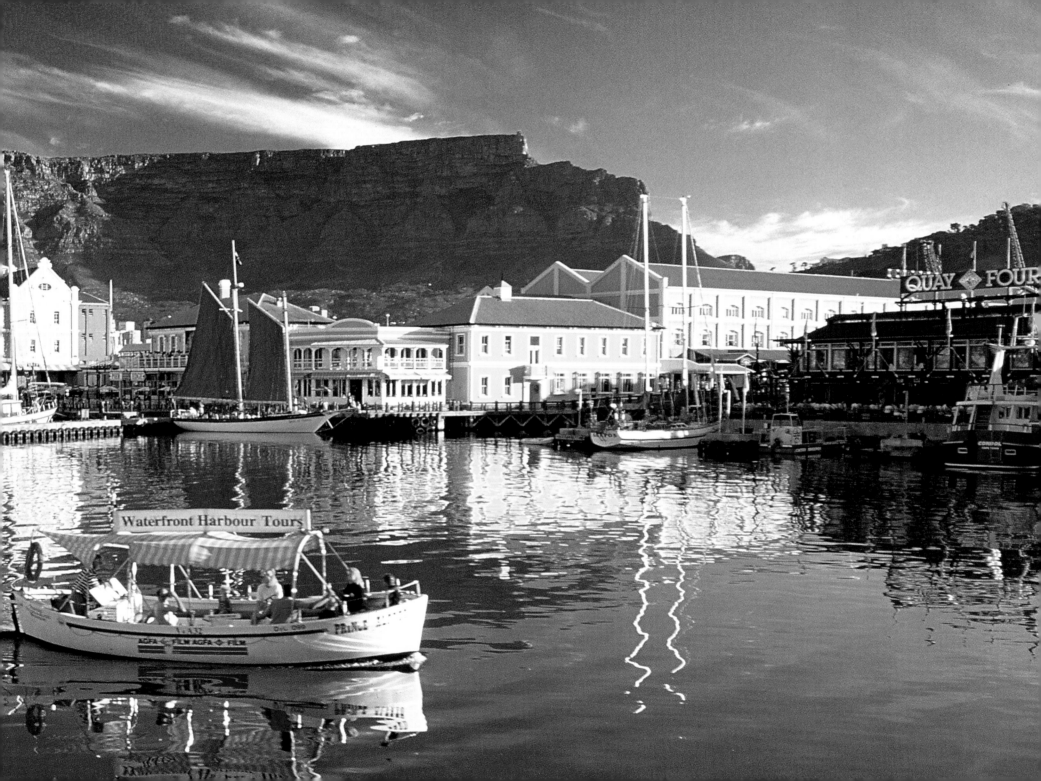

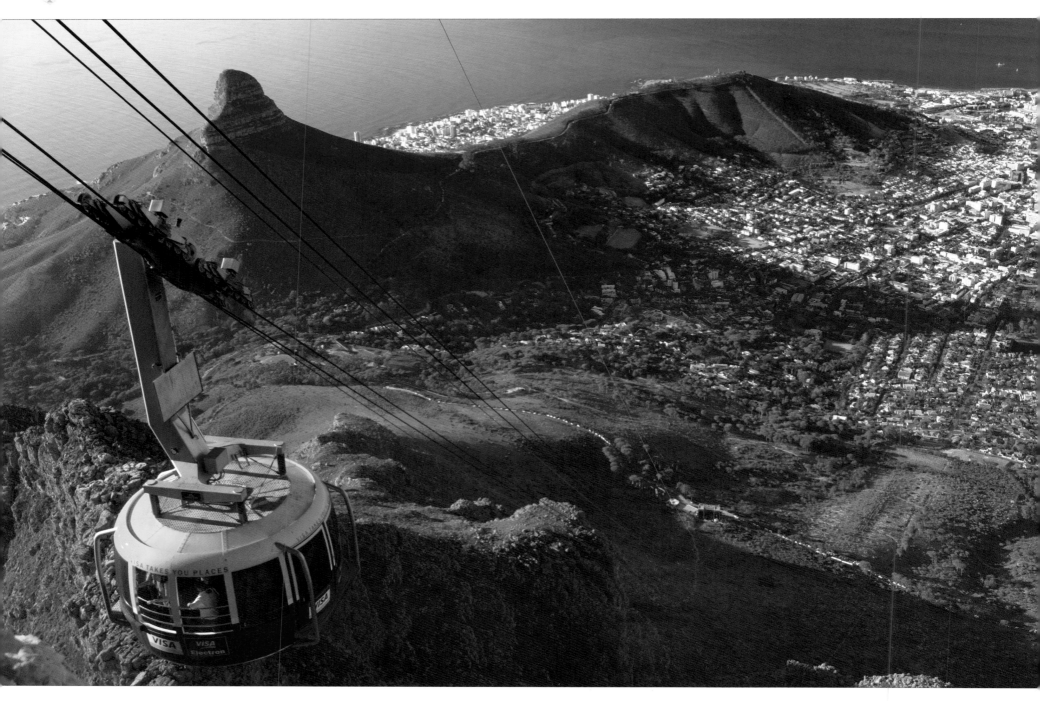

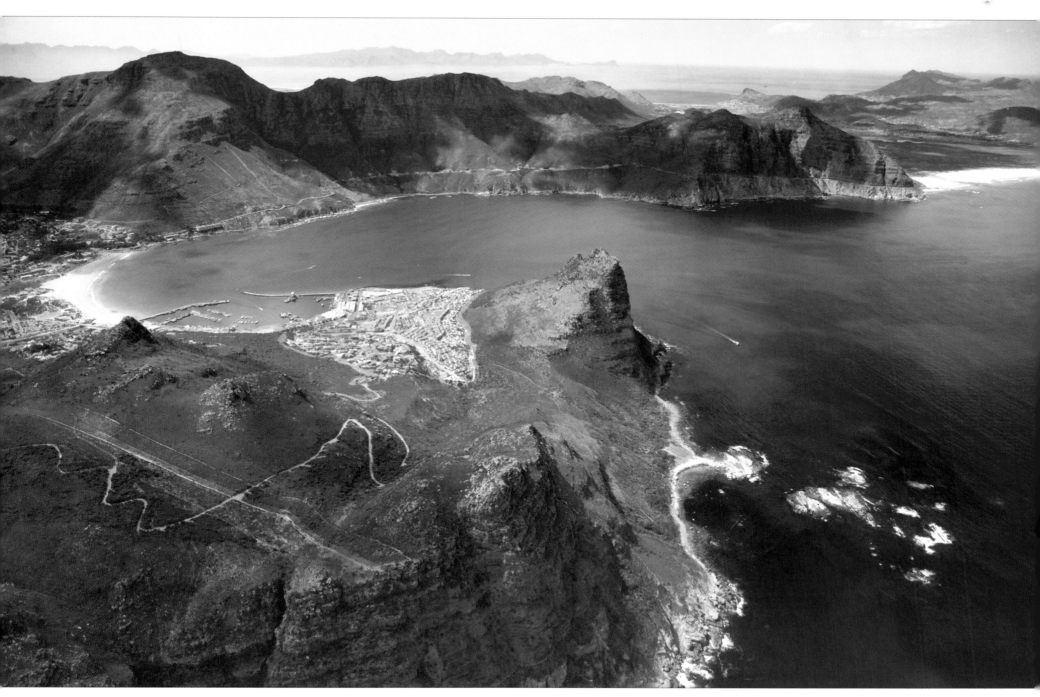

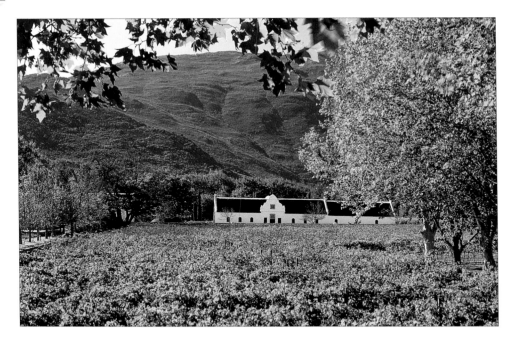

PREVIOUS PAGE, LEFT Ever since early European seafarers set eyes on Table Mountain, which forms the impressive backdrop to the Cape, visitors have clambered to its flat-topped summit. Today, the modern cable-car system continues to ferry holidaymakers and locals to the top, offering magnificent views over the thriving city below and beyond to the Hottentots-Holland mountains.

PREVIOUS PAGE, RIGHT Many of the early settlements at the Cape Colony started life as small, rustic stations harbouring villagers who eked a living from the land they occupied. Today, while many have grown into large urban conurbations, the people of the self-styled 'Republic of Hout Bay' continue to cling to a simpler way of life and the suburb has retained much of its original charm.

ABOVE The La Motte wine estate, in the very heart of the Cape Winelands, is one of the region's finest, most established and most acclaimed wine producers. With a long and proud history of viticulture dating back to when the Huguenots first planted their stock in Cape soil, many of the latter-day enterprises are both modern and sophisticated, utilising the very latest technology to produce some of the country's finest wines.

OPPOSITE Although South Africa first earned a reputation for its fine wine as a result of the vines planted on the Peninsula itself, the industry rapidly began to extend far beyond the immediate confines of Constantia to as far afield as Stellenbosch, where the wine production initiated by its early French settlers is now a prime income-earner for the Cape hinterland.

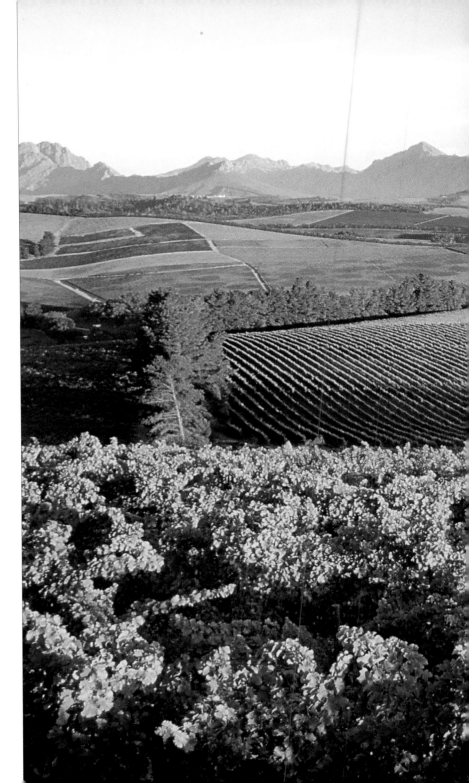

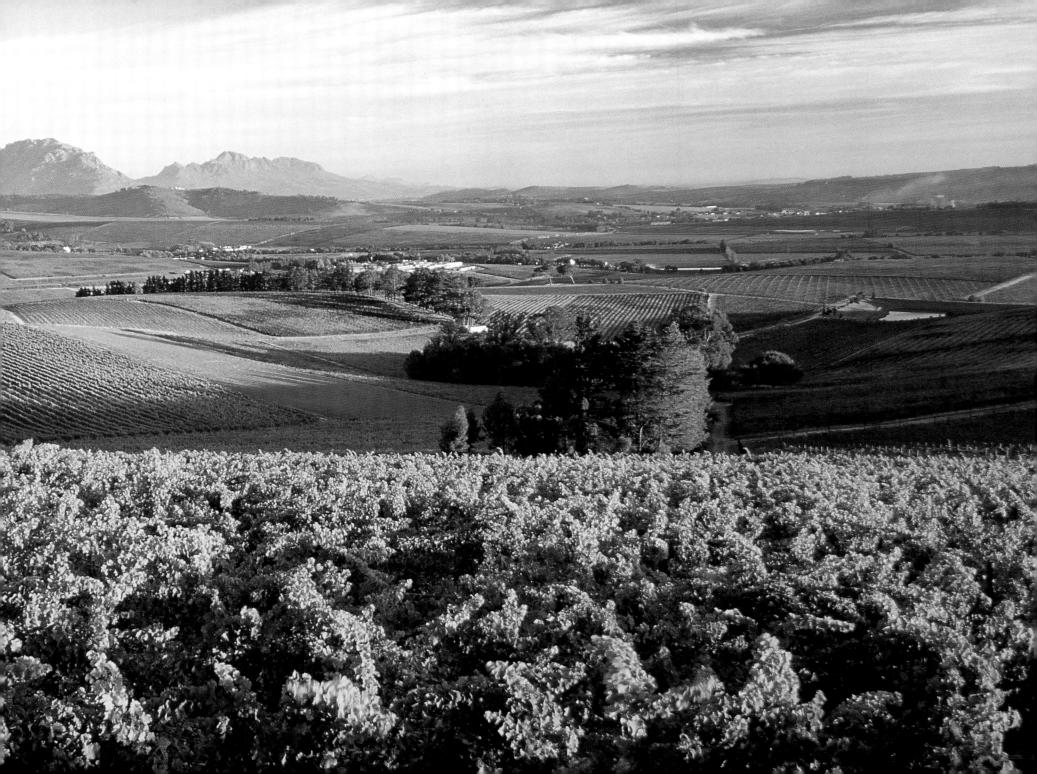

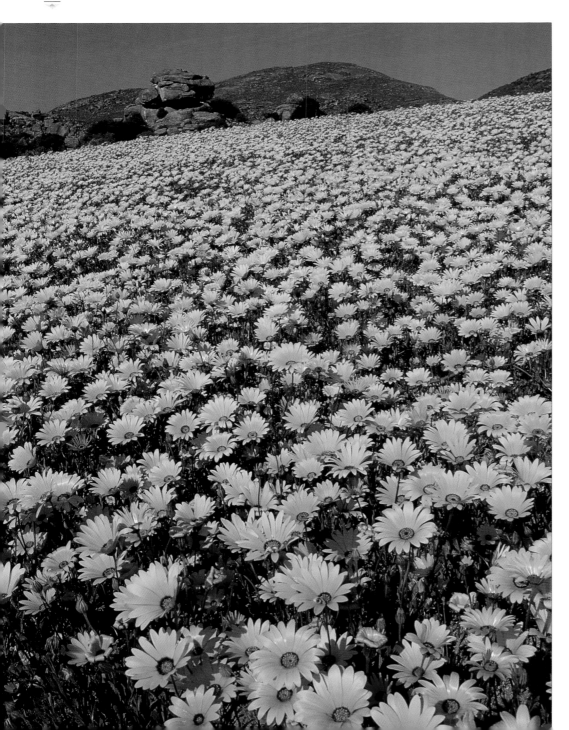

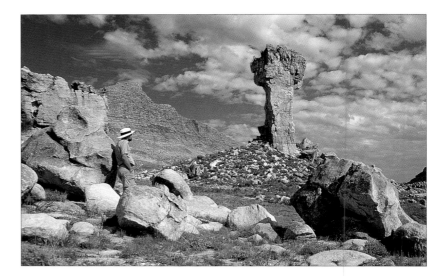

LEFT AND OPPOSITE In an area that consists mostly of the empty space that is the Great Karoo, much of the Northern Cape is dry and dusty, with few signs of life – either floral or faunal. The view, however, is generally deceiving. In spring, with the fall of the early rains, vast stretches of Namaqualand burst into flower, with species such as the famed Namaqualand daisy taking pride of place. The rocky shrubland of Namaqualand can look quite barren, especially in the dry months, but with the emergence of these flowers the vast fields of what is little more than stone and sand are transformed. This extraordinary revival of colour continues to prove a major attraction to the area, and visitors from all across the globe flock here in August and September when the flowers are at their most spectacular.

TOP The dramatic rock formation commonly known as the Maltese Cross is one of the principal landmarks of the Cederberg, an area of the Western Cape that boasts a number of equally striking natural features, among them the Wolfberg Cracks and the Wolfberg Arch. Because the region is scarcely populated and apparently inhospitable, much of it remains unspoilt wilderness, attracting hikers, trailists and other keen adventurers to its desolate landscape. Today, there are a number of established trails for both hikers and mountain bikers, for example.

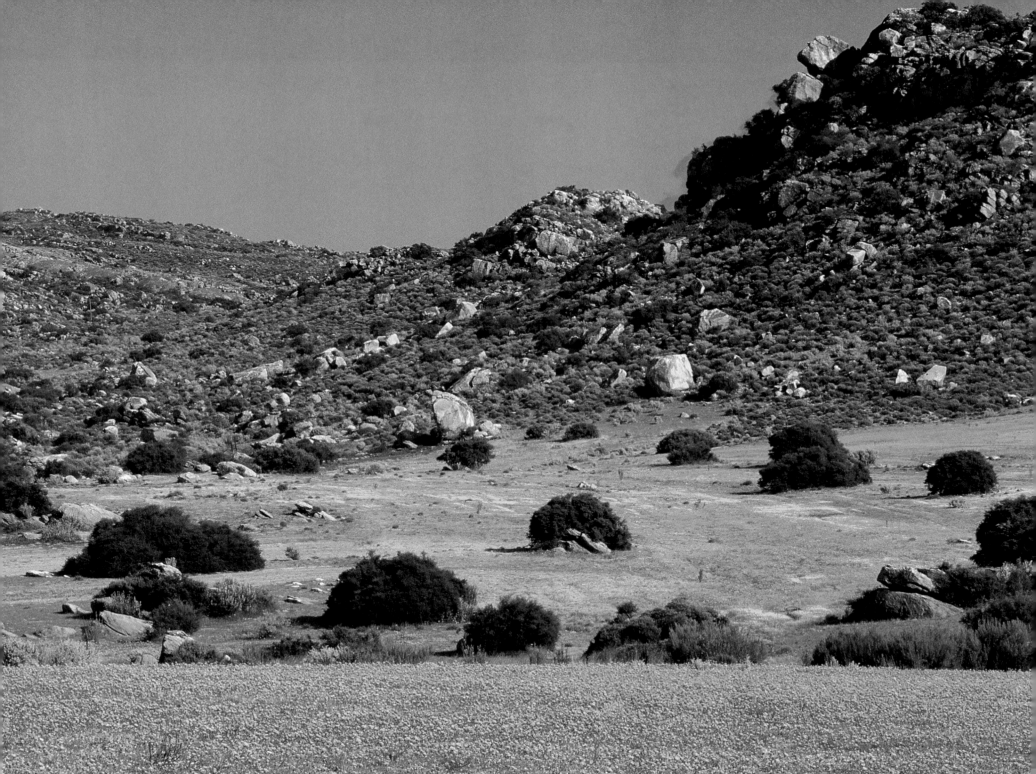

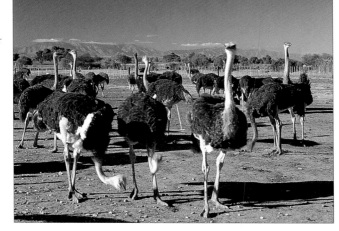

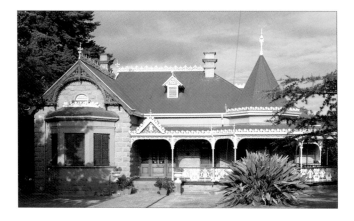

TOP AND RIGHT The rather harsh climate of the Little Karoo –
the hinterland of the southern Cape enclosed by the Witberg,
Swartberg, Langeberg and Outeniqua mountains are not
conducive to extensive crop plantations. They are, however, ideal
for the rearing of ostriches, hardy birds accustomed to the hot,
dry conditions.

ABOVE In the late 1800s and early 1900s, when ostrich feathers
were a popular fashion accessory worldwide, ostrich-rearing proved
an extremely lucrative enterprise and many local farmers, reaping
great benefits, built lavish homes.

OVERLEAF In the Overberg, just beyond the Hottentots-Holland
mountains, much of the cultivated land is planted with canola,
the vibrant yellow covering much of the roadside along the N2
highway, for example.

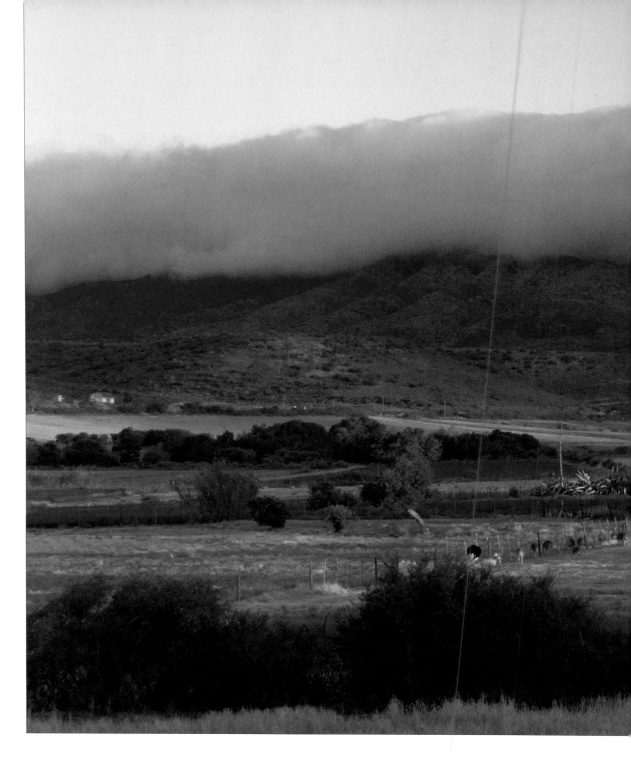

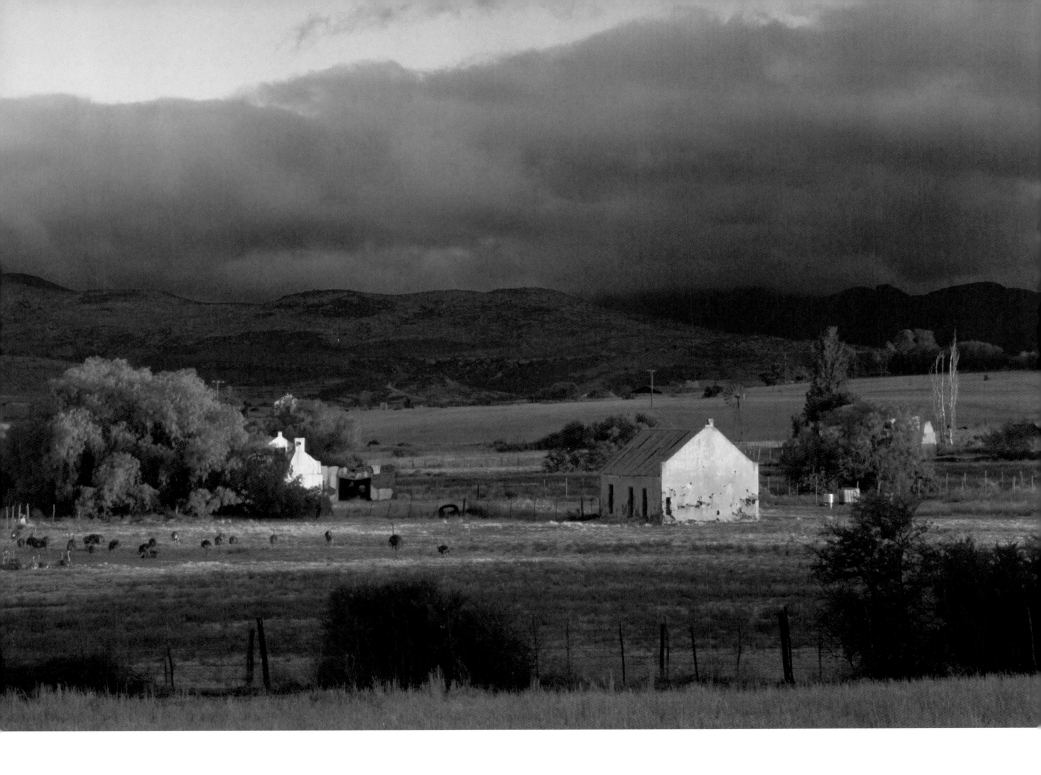

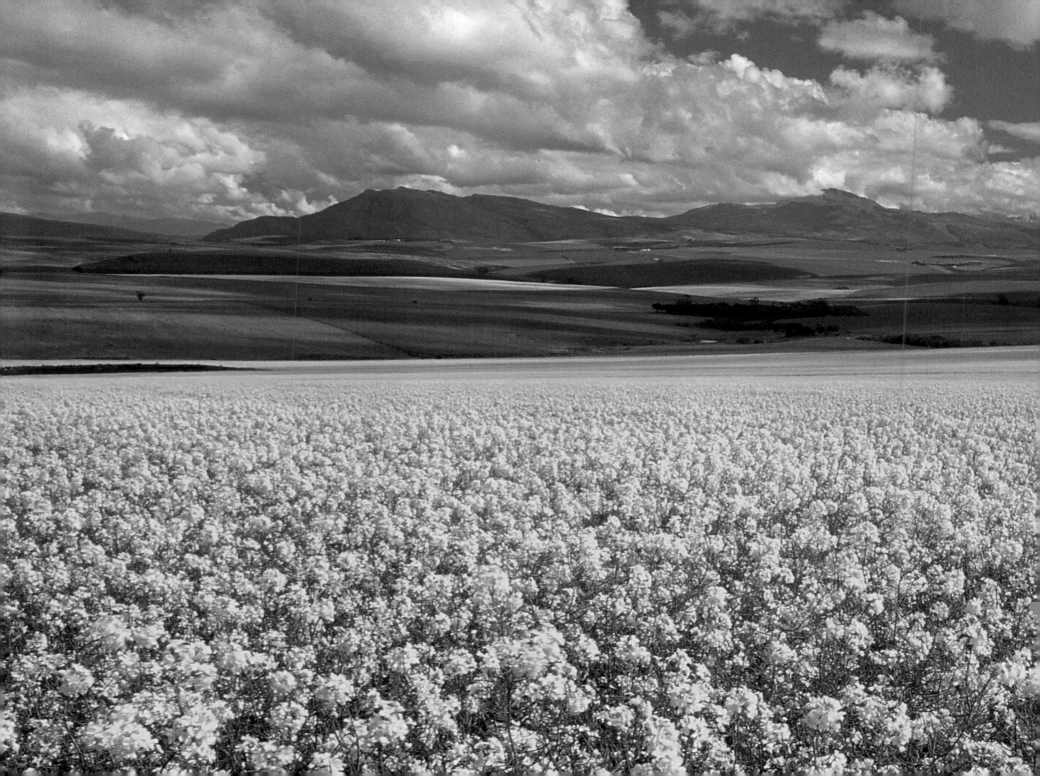

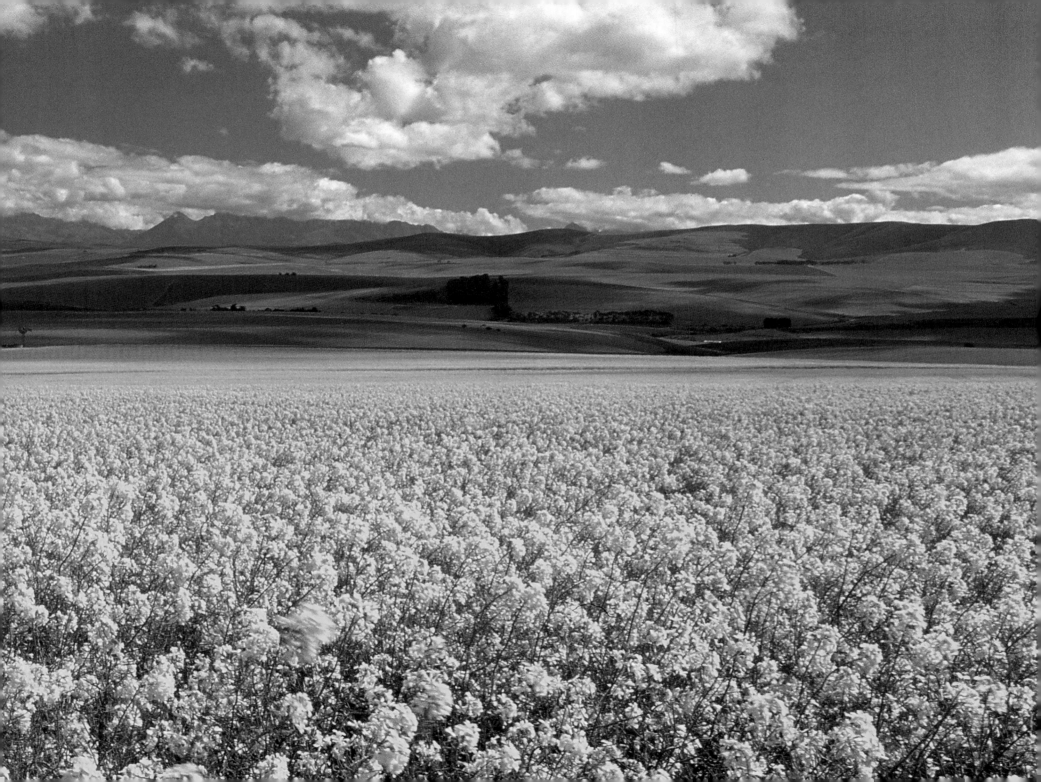

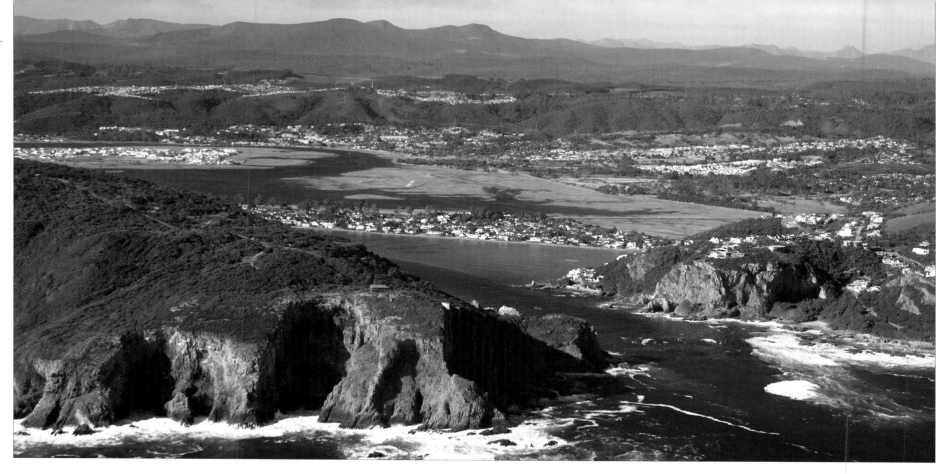

ABOVE The seaside town of Knysna – along with its neighbour Plettenberg Bay just to the north – has become one of the Cape's premier holiday destinations. Situated on the scenic Garden Route, which extends from about Heidelberg in the south to the mouth of Storms River, the pretty little settlement situated between the foothills of the Outeniqua mountains and the shores of the Indian Ocean is most noted for the lagoon that forms its focal point and The Heads, the looming buttresses that guard the town.

RIGHT The rather sleepy town of George is the proud seat of one of the country's most acclaimed golf courses, the luxurious Fancourt Golf Estate and Country Club, playground of famous golfers who have reached the pinnacle of success on international circuits.

OPPOSITE The bridge that spans the Storms River, which cuts through the Tsitsikamma forest reserve, stands nearly 40 metres (130 feet) above the flowing water. The river itself originates in the high wetlands of the natural forest, which in turn takes its name, Tsitsikamma, from the Khoi word meaning 'running water'.

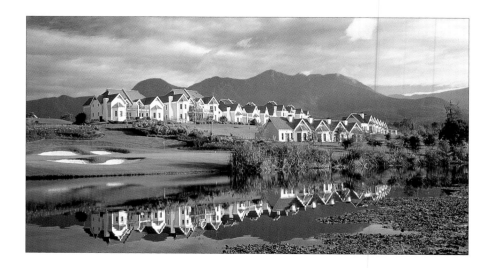

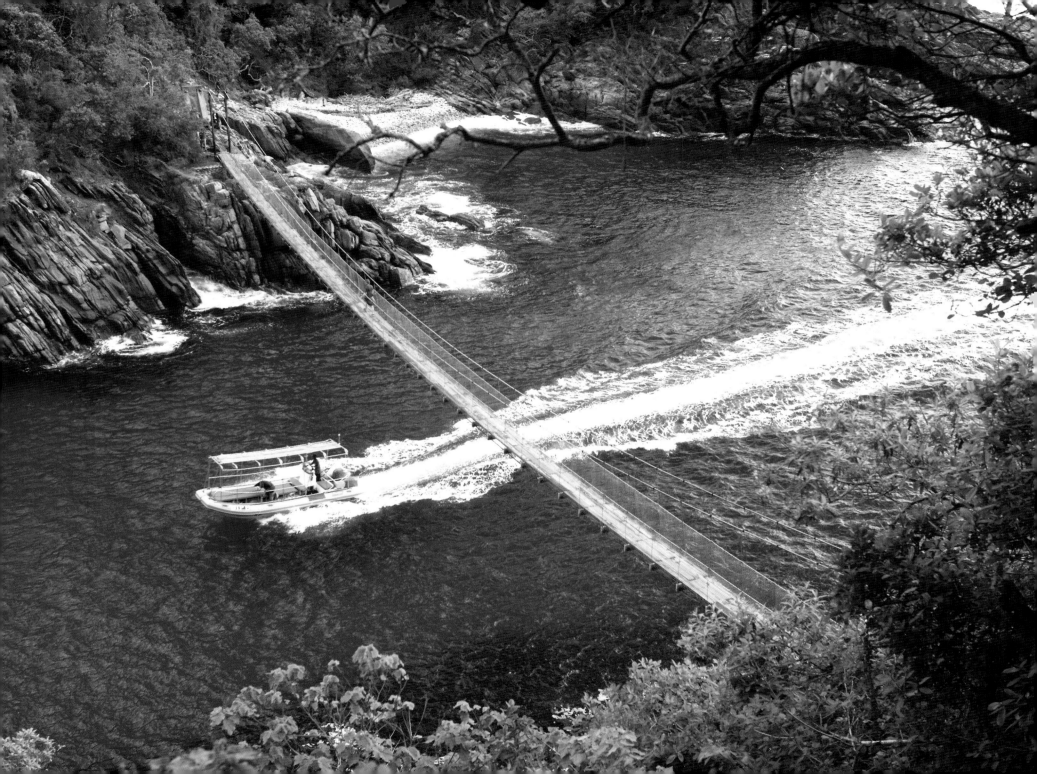

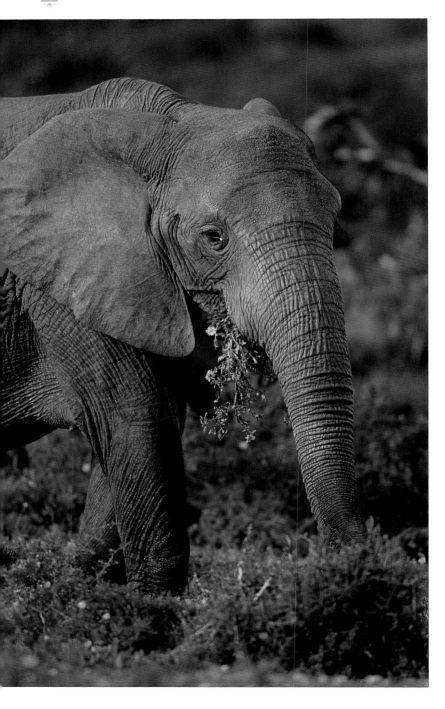

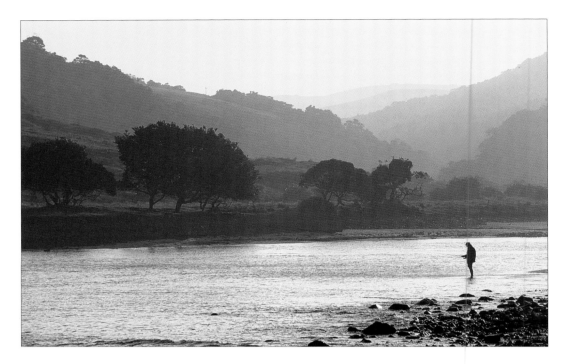

LEFT Although the Big Five once roamed freely across much of the country, including the eastern seaboard, wildlife in the Eastern Cape is now generally limited to birds – of which there are abundant species – and the smaller mammals. That said, however, reserves such as Shamwari, widely acclaimed as one of the finest in the world, have reintroduced many of the big game species into the region. It is, however, the elephants of the Greater Addo Elephant National Park, just north of Port Elizabeth, that remain the region's primary wildlife experience.

ABOVE The Eastern Cape and, more specifically, the shoreline commonly referred to as the Wild Coast, is an especially scenic area. While much of the interior suffers periodically from often debilitating drought, the coastal area is generally verdant, the tumultous Indian Ocean fed by the tranquil lagoons and seasonal rivers that spill into the rough seas here.

OPPOSITE Addo has its elephants, Shamwari its lion, and the Mountain Zebra National Park – on the mountain slopes of the Bankberg near Cradock – its Cape mountain zebra. Facing near-extinction, or certainly rapidly dwindling numbers in the first half of the twentieth century, a special reserve was established in order to protect local populations. Today thriving herds are well established among the vegetation of largely sweet-thorn and karee species, living side by side with lynx, caracal and antelope species such as black wildebeest, eland, springbok and duiker.

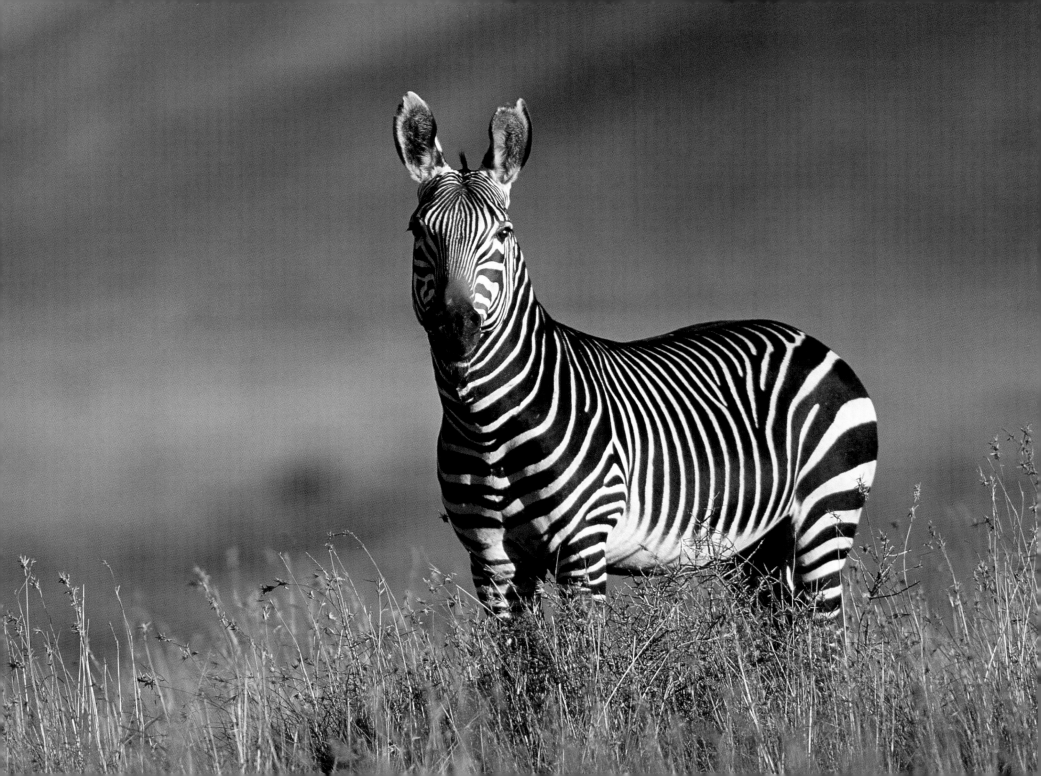

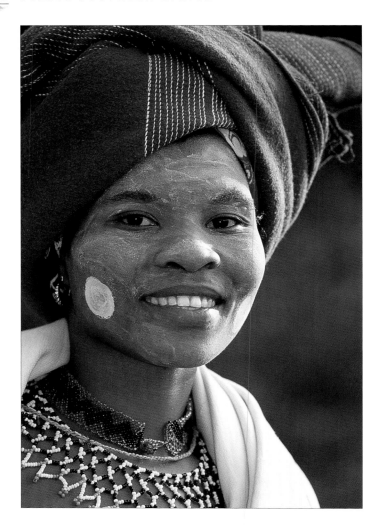

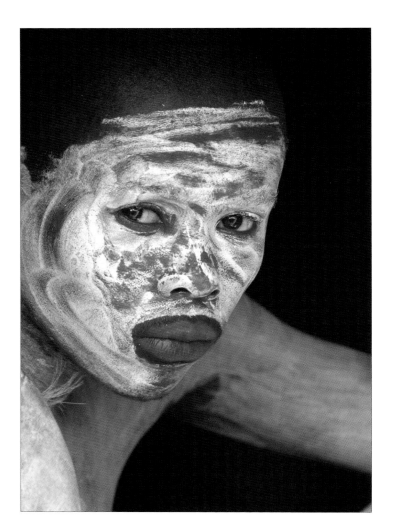

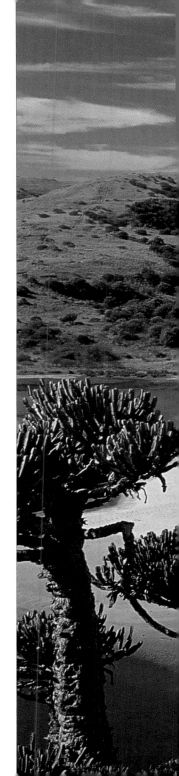

ABOVE AND TOP RIGHT The rural Eastern Cape is the traditional home of the Xhosa. According to tradition, Xhosa women (above) are the home makers and tillers of the soil, the men warriors and hunters. At certain times of the year, the *amaKwetha* – young boys who are circumcised in the initiation rites that signify their transition to manhood – still conduct the ceremonies passed down by their forefathers.

OPPOSITE In stark contrast to the tranquil rural scenes so much a feature of the interior, the shoreline of the Eastern Cape, although gentle at times, is best known for the volatility that earned it the name of the Wild Coast.
OVERLEAF The foothills of KwaZulu-Natal's Drakensberg – or *uKhahlamba*, the name by which the local Zulu people know the great 'barrier of spears' – boast what is probably the most scenic backdrop in all South Africa.

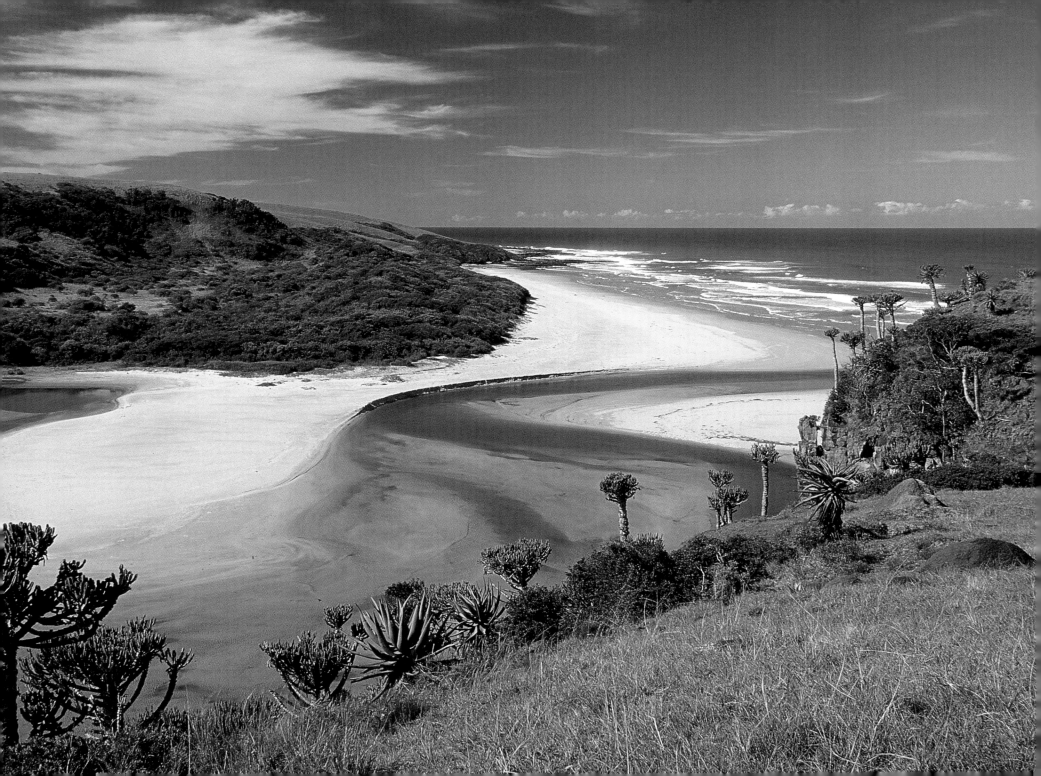

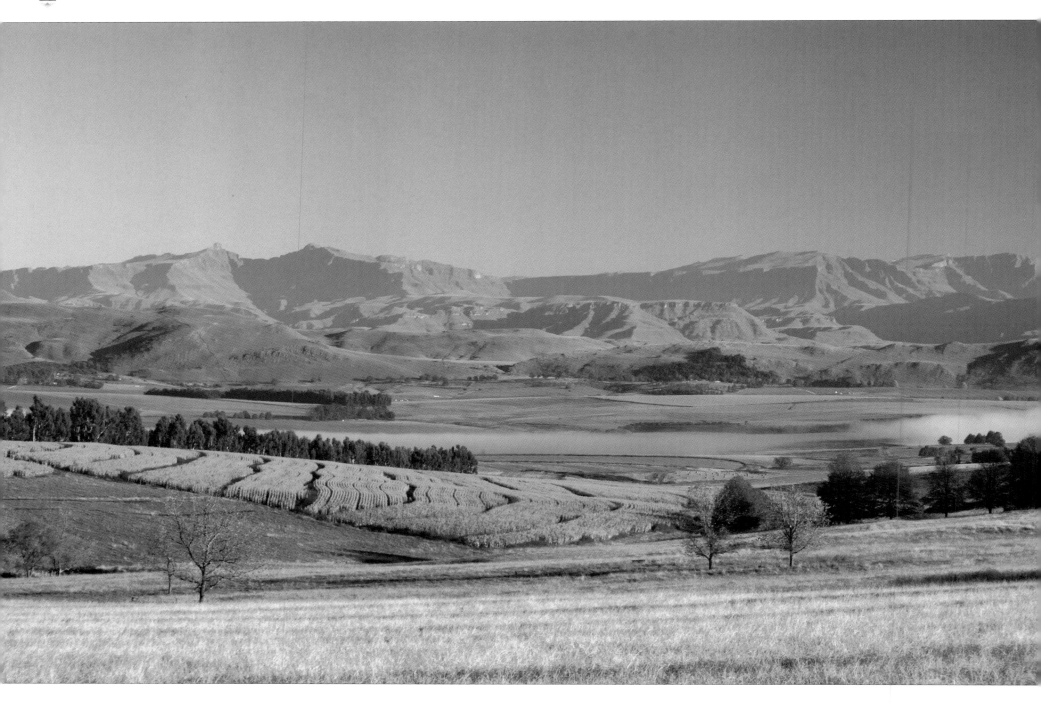

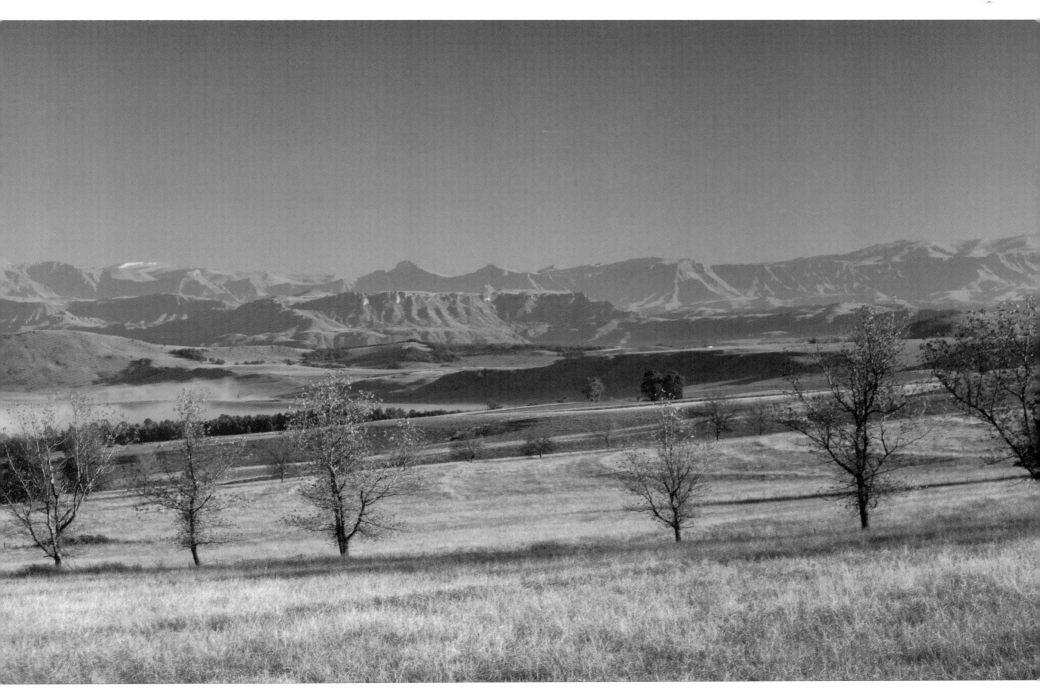

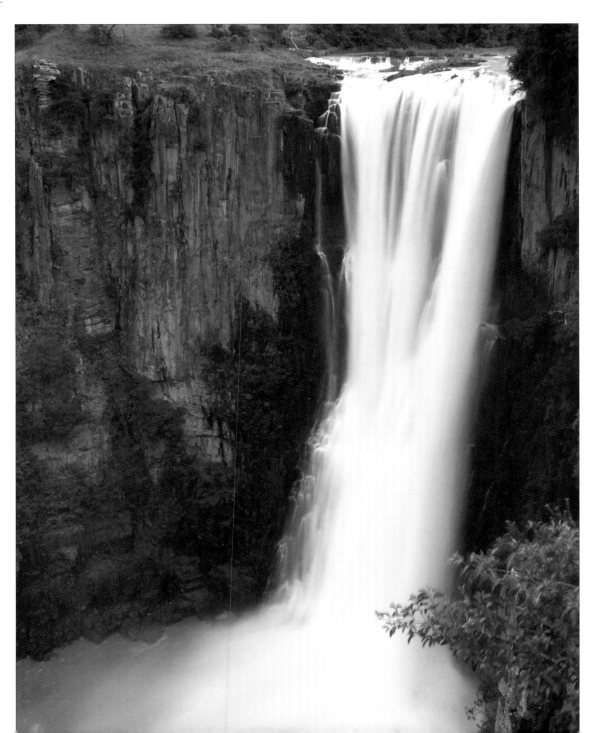

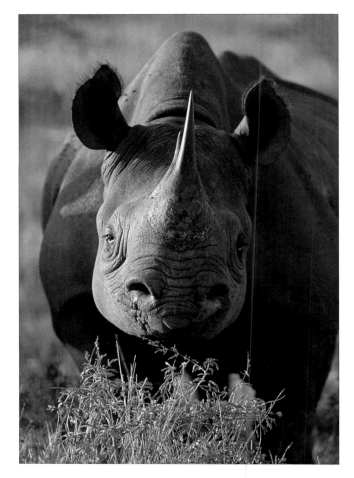

LEFT Because so much of KwaZulu-Natal is mountainous, the midlands and foothills are home to a number of important water courses. One of the most significant is the Mgeni River, along which one finds the scenic Howick Falls.

ABOVE Mkuze Game Reserve remains one of KwaZulu-Natal's – and, indeed, South Africa's – finest, and boasts a proud history of conservation, one of its great success stories being the restoration of local populations of the black rhino.

OPPOSITE The Kosi Bay Nature Reserve, situated at the mouth of the bay that shares its name, comprises a series of pristine lakes, swamps and estuaries.

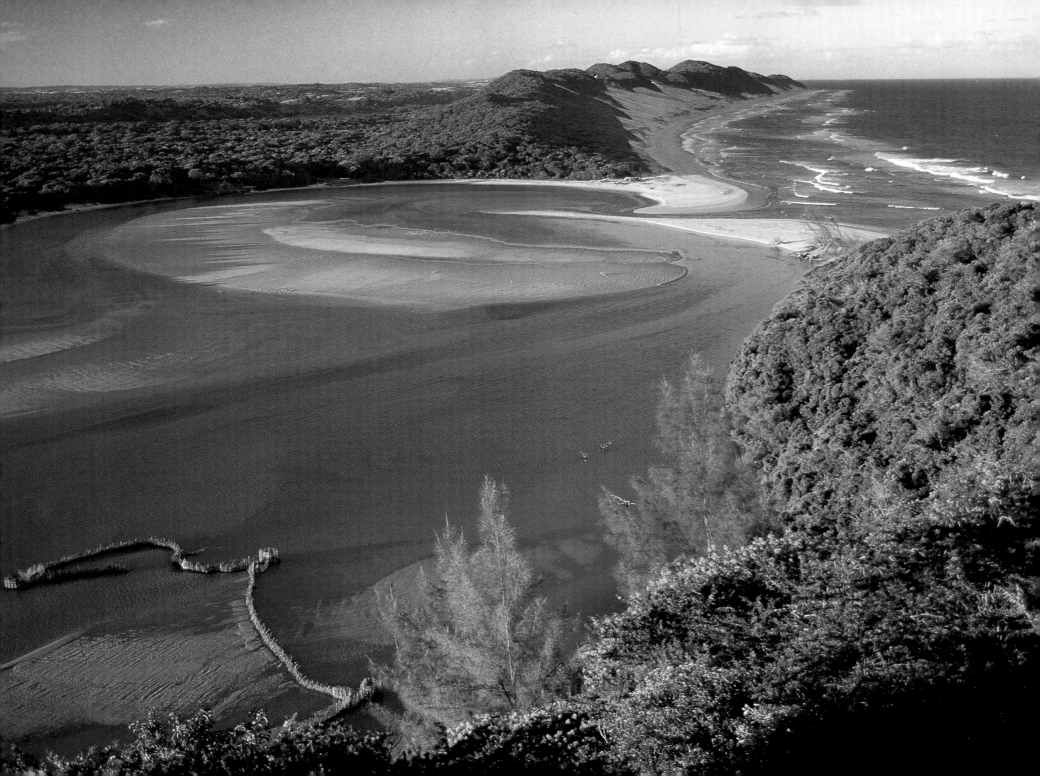

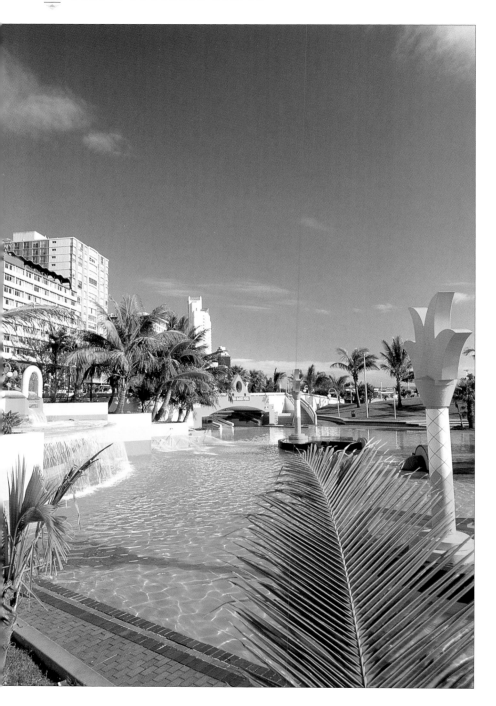

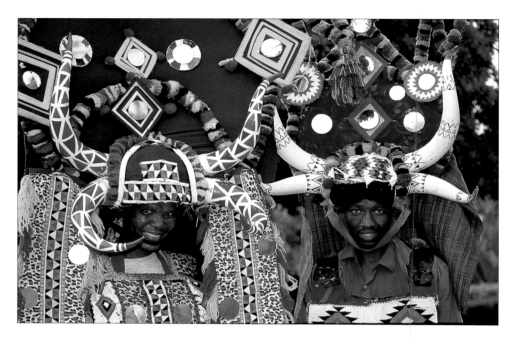

LEFT Durban's popular marina and beachfront, splashes of colour on a picturesque coastline, cater well for the all-important tourism network that incorporates the city beaches as well as the leisure strips of both the north and south coasts.

ABOVE KwaZulu-Natal is the traditional home of the Zulu people, many of whom still lead largely rural lives in the province's hilly green interior and beyond. Ricksha pullers, however, trace their origins to the colonial era, when they fulfilled an important transport function.

OPPOSITE Because it is situated on a large natural harbour, Durban has always been an important port settlement and, while the city now boasts a modern and sophisticated infrastructure, life for many locals continues to revolve around the Indian Ocean and the livelihood it offers.

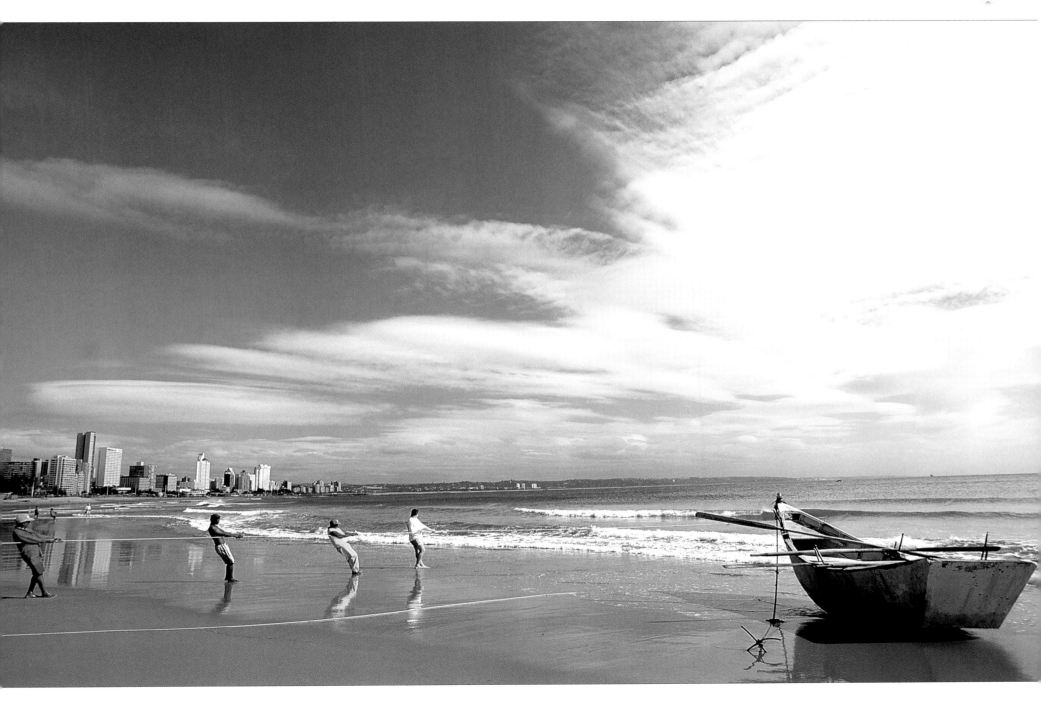

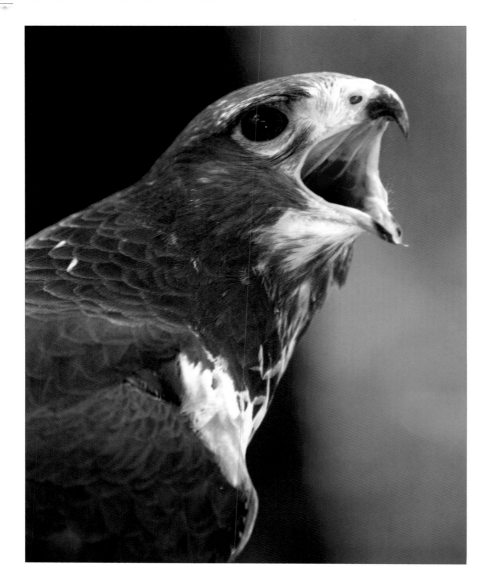

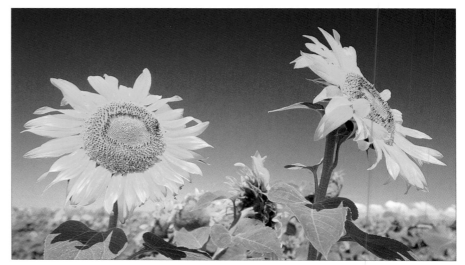

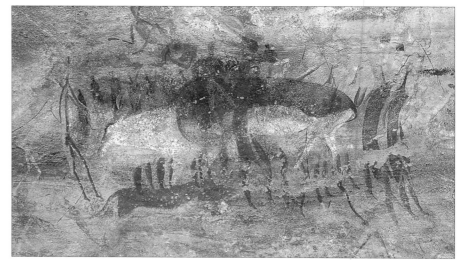

ABOVE Central South Africa, even the relatively dry plains of, for example, the Free State, are prime birding territory, where birds of prey such as the jackal buzzard have made their home.
TOP RIGHT Parts of the Free State, such as the Senekal area, are given over to sunflower farming.
ABOVE CENTRE The Tandjiesberg Cave near Ladybrand in the Free State is widely acknowledged as one of the most significant San art sites in the country.

OPPOSITE The Free State borders the small independent kingdom of Lesotho, the traditional home of the Basotho people. Although the nation is now scattered throughout much of South Africa, the people of the area still practise traditional arts and crafts such as weaving, beadwork and mural painting, and many still follow the distinctly rural way of life depicted at the Basotho Cultural Village.

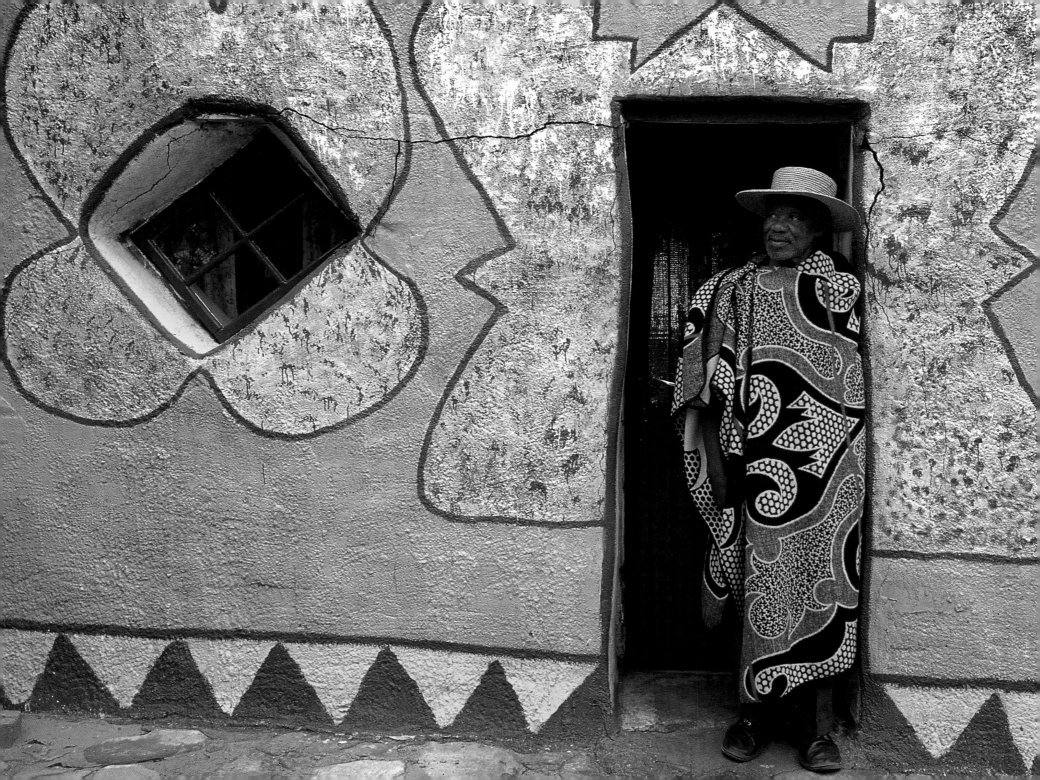

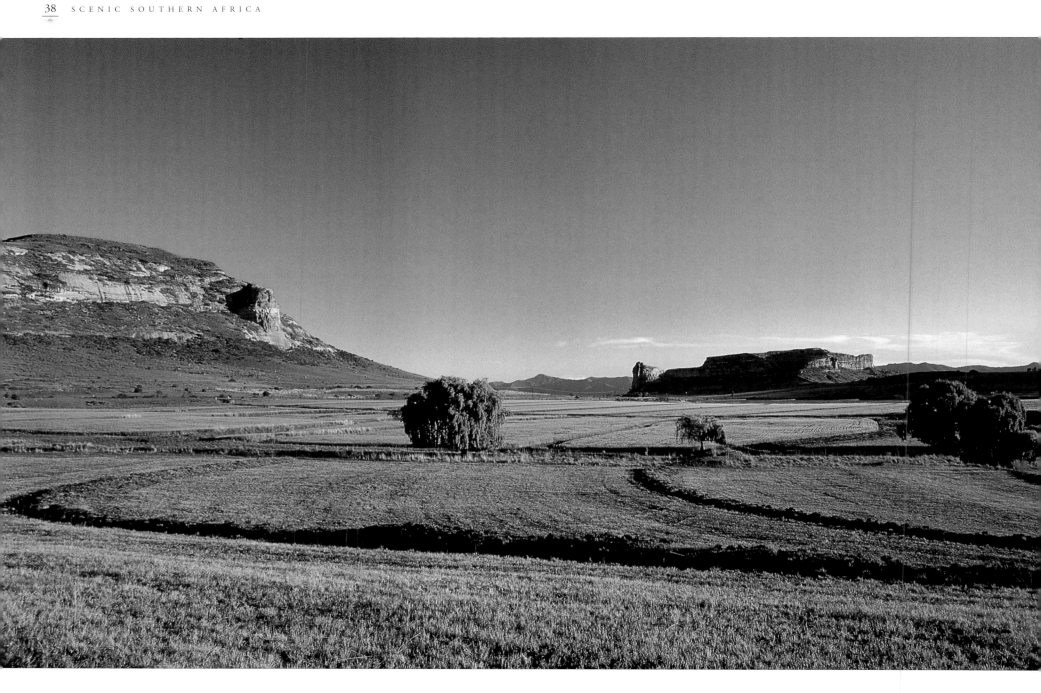

ABOVE Much of the Free State is under cultivation and the province's all-important wheatfields mean that it is generally considered South Africa's 'bread basket'.

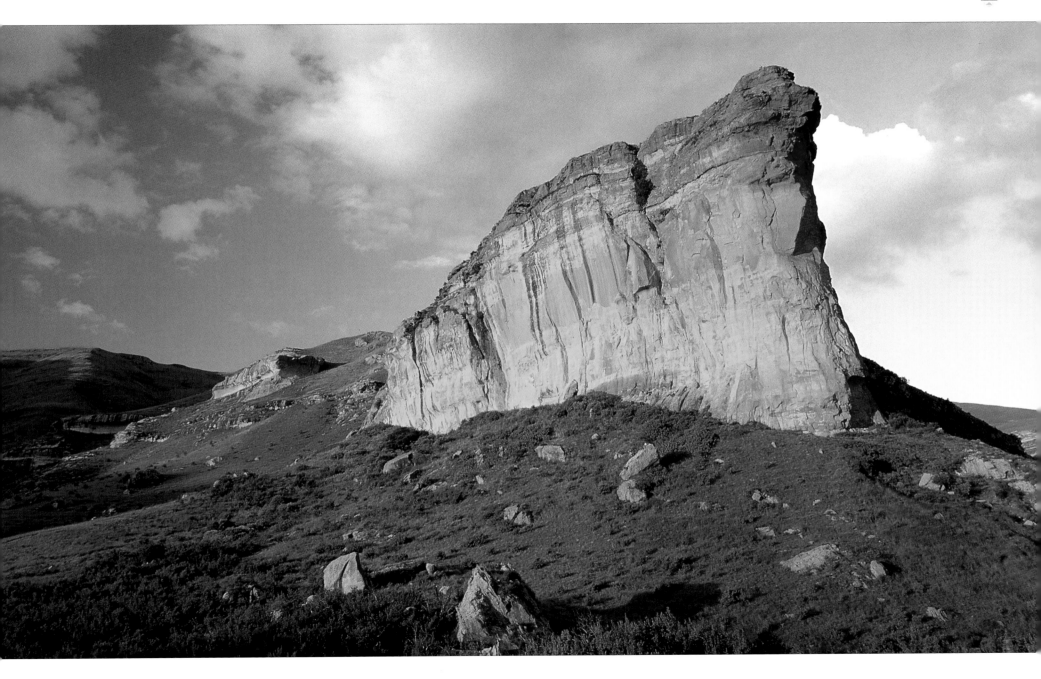

ABOVE The Brandwag is the most enduring face of the Free State's Golden Gate Highlands National Park, the province's chief conservation area.

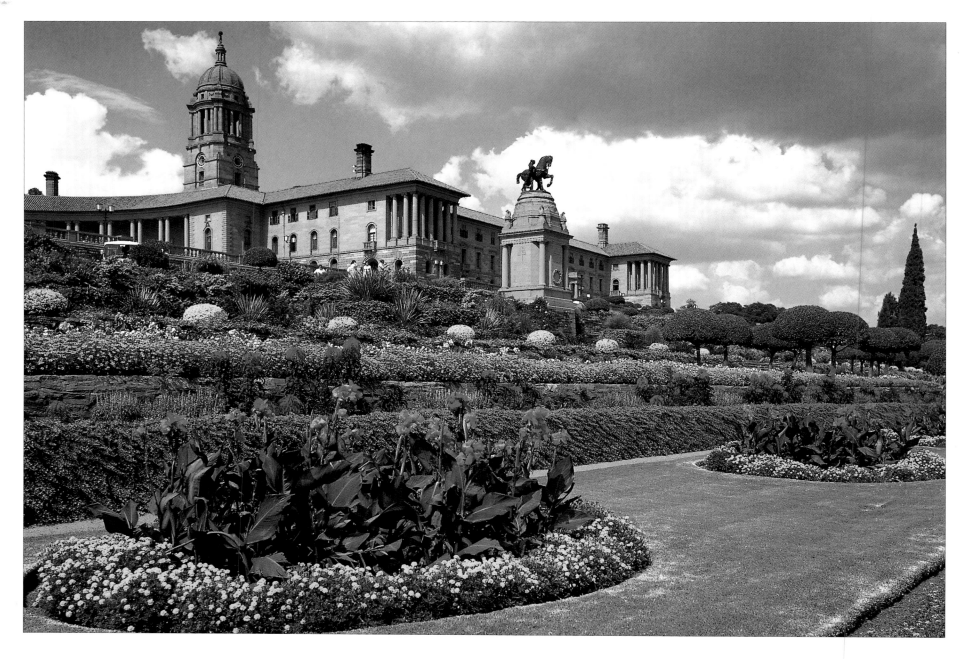

ABOVE Although Pretoria's Union Buildings were where apartheid was conceived, it remains the primary seat of government in democratic South Africa.

OPPOSITE Metropolitan Johannesburg, the City of Gold and the heart of Gauteng, is South Africa's most significant centre, a First World city in every respect.

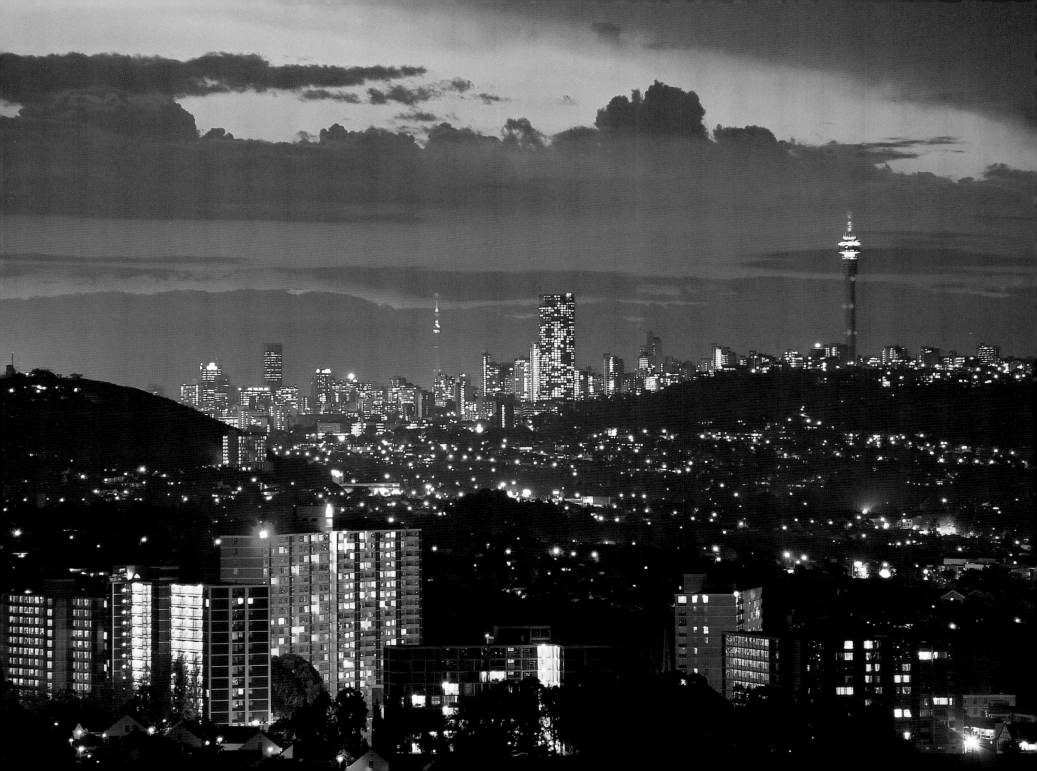

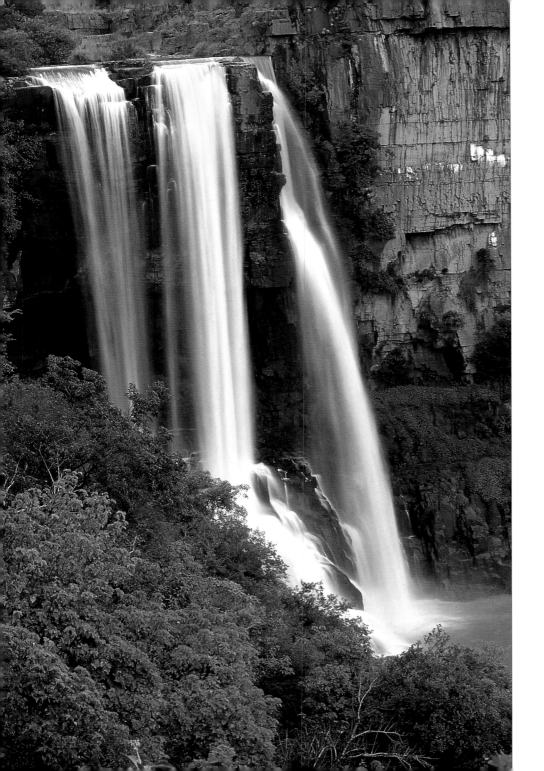

LEFT Mpumalanga is blessed with a wide network of water courses – some small, others significant – that transforms vast stretches of the rocky countryside into a thickly vegetated and extremely green wonderland. It is here, near Waterval-Boven, on what is commonly referred to as the Waterfall Route, that the attractive Elands River Falls are found.

BELOW AND OPPOSITE, RIGHT Large parts of the forested mountain slopes of the Mpumalanga Escarpment are interlaced with crystal-clear rivers and streams that feed the rich and densely covered soils. This wooded landscape at Lone Creek Falls, near Sabie, is typical of the features of the broader region.

OPPOSITE TOP LEFT In the shadow of Mount Anderson, one of the region's tallest peaks – some 2 285 metres (7 495 feet) above sea level – lies the Mount Anderson Ranch near the town of Lydenburg, heartland of Mpumalanga's prime trout-fishing country.

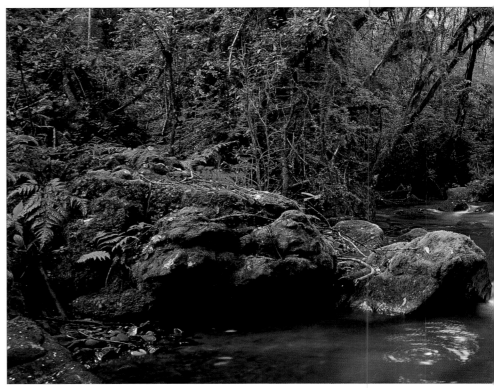

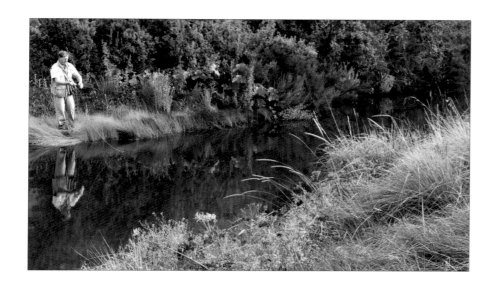

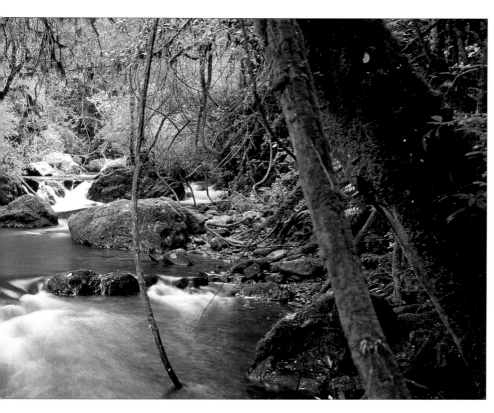

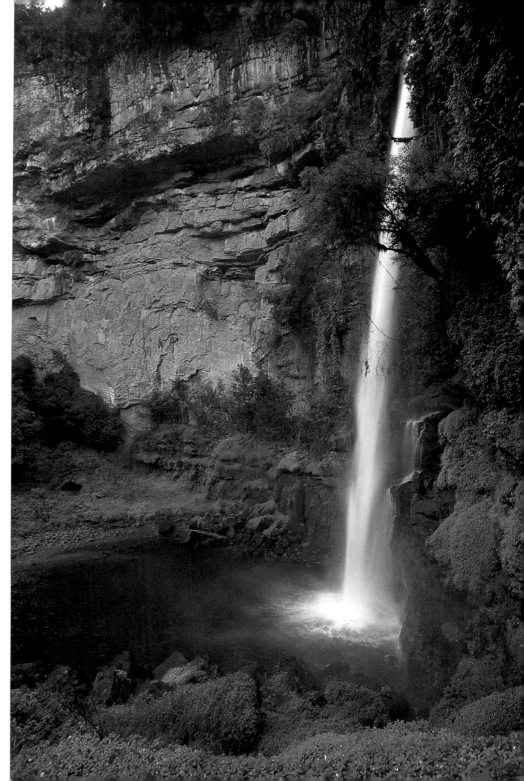

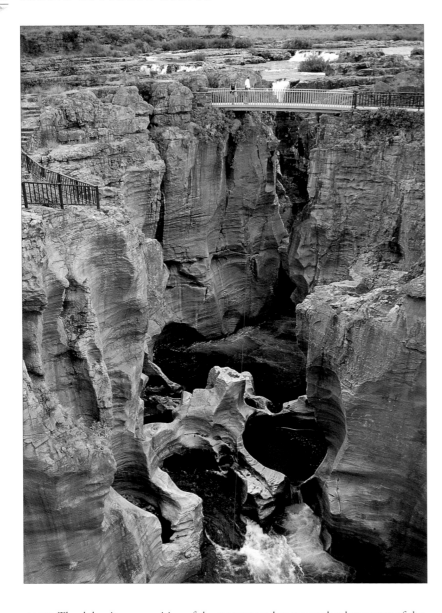

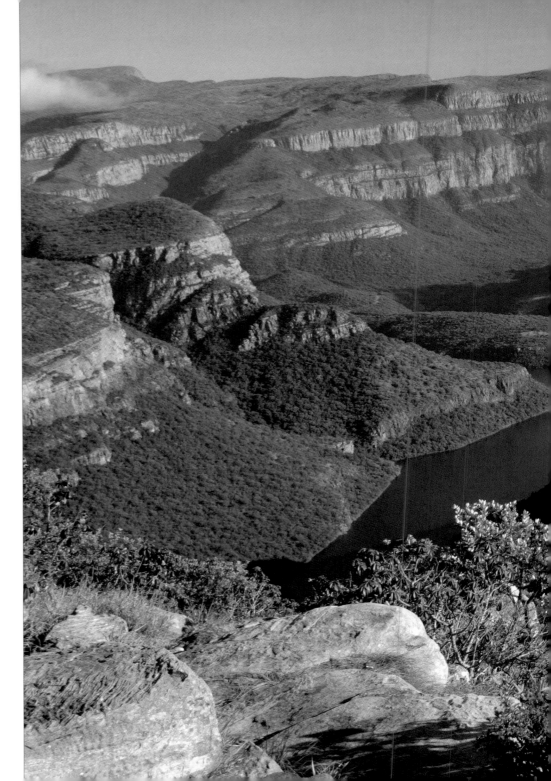

ABOVE The dolomite composition of the escarpment has meant that large parts of the terrain are susceptible to corrosion and this, combined with the effects of the moving waters of the Treur and Blyde rivers, have etched the famed Bourke's Luck Potholes. RIGHT The view from the Blyde River platform extends across the Canyon and over the dam to the Lowveld.

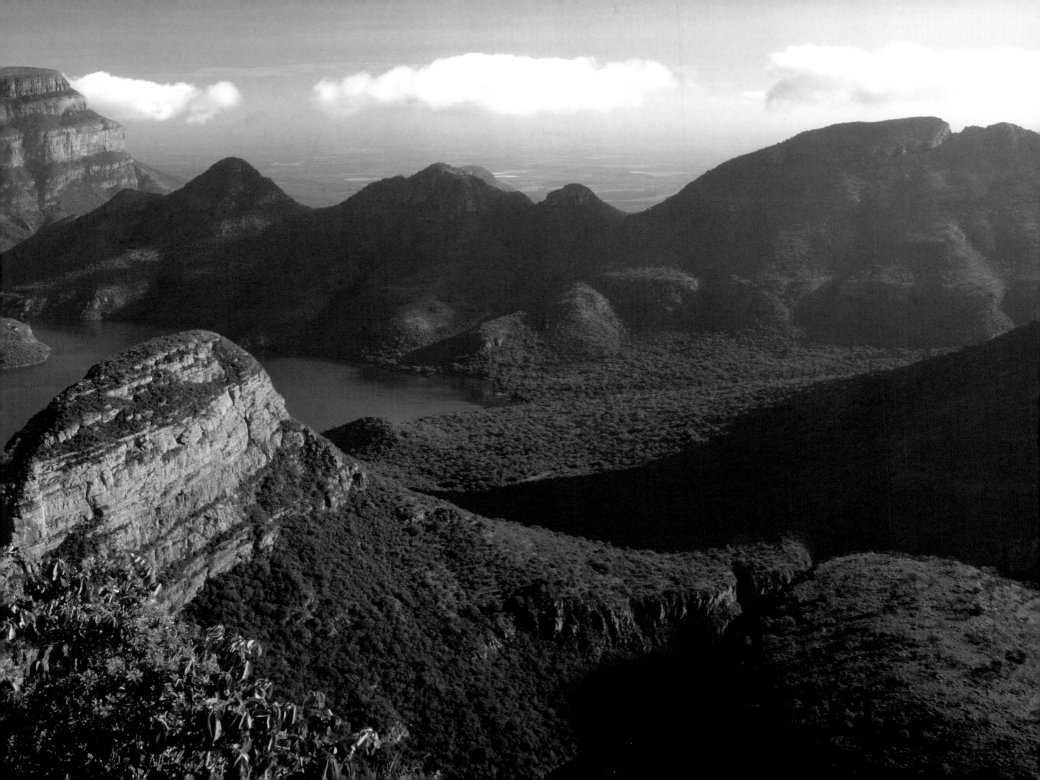

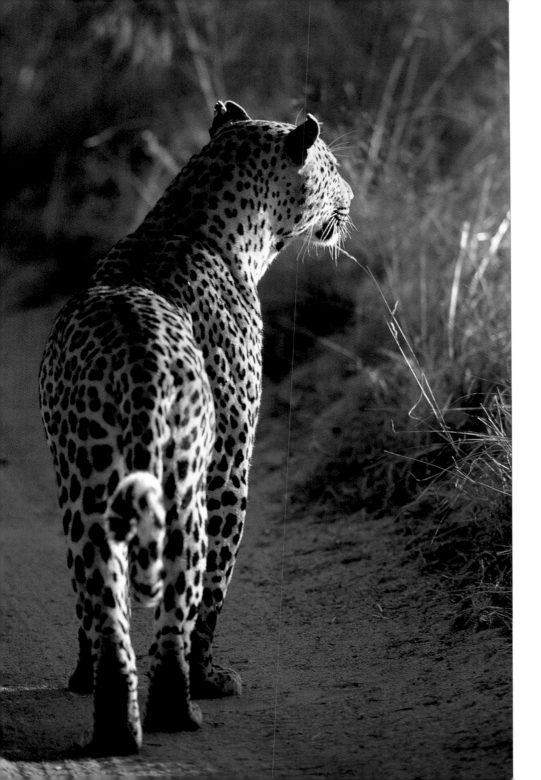

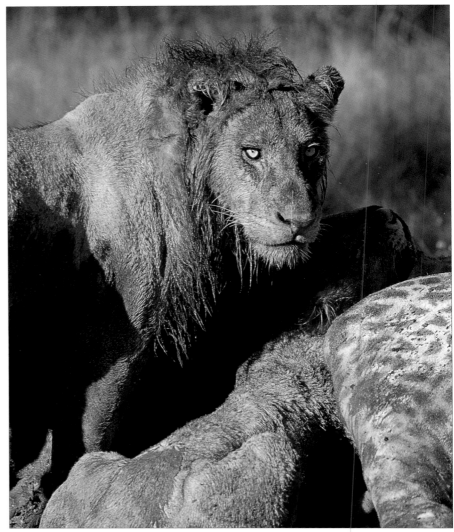

LEFT The northeastern parts of the country comprise mostly bushveld, the big-game country of the Kruger and smaller private reserves, most notably Mala Mala, which is most famous for its thriving leopard population.

ABOVE The Kruger National Park boasts all of the Big Five, king of which is the lion, Africa's largest cat and one that was once found throughout much of the country.

OPPOSITE Kruger is also home to African elephant, the beast perhaps most often associated with the northern bushveld.

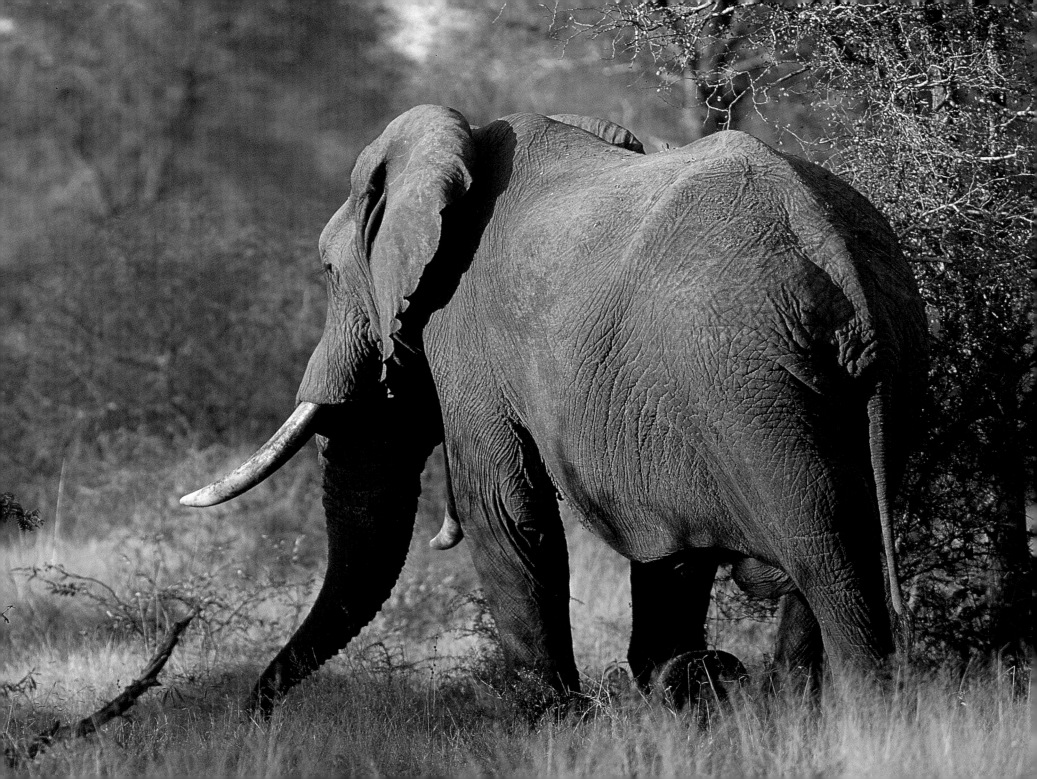

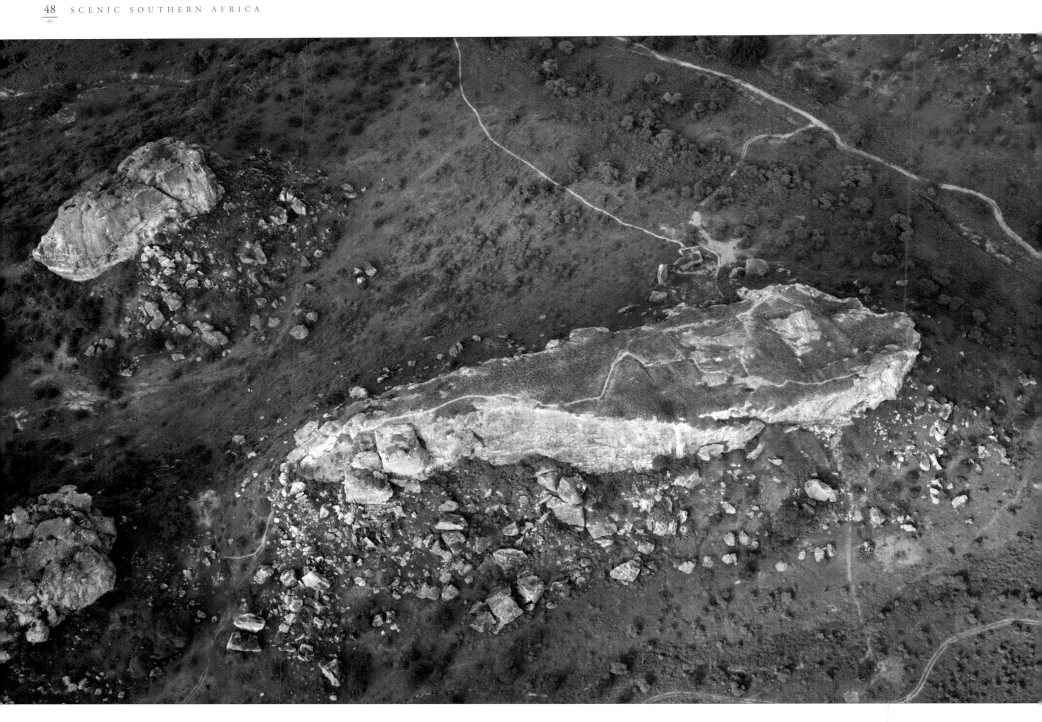

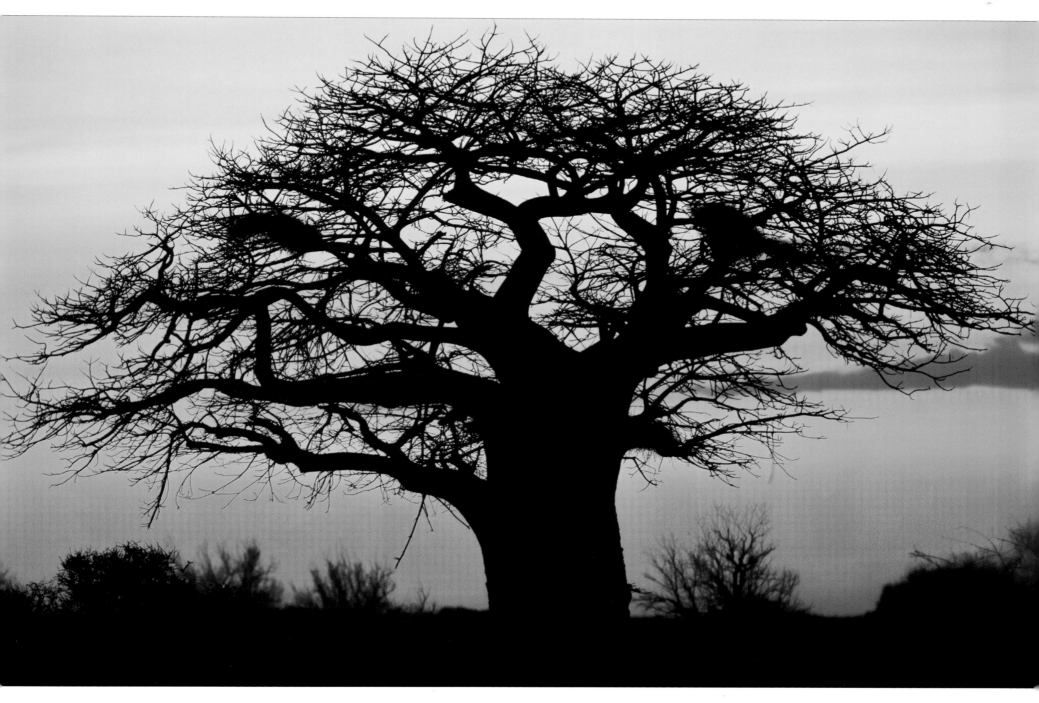

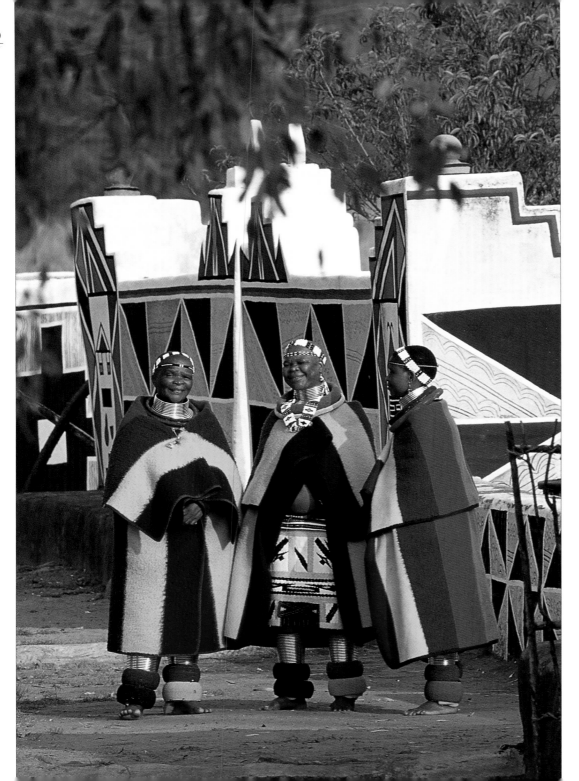

PREVIOUS PAGE, LEFT The ancient ruins of Mapungubwe, in the far northern corner of Limpopo Province, is an archaeological treasure that showcases South Africa's oldest civilisation.

PREVIOUS PAGE, RIGHT The northern regions of the Limpopo province are best known for their majestic baobabs.

LEFT, BELOW AND OPPOSITE The Ndebele people, traditional inhabitants of the northern regions for centuries, are today best known for the remarkable aesthetic value of their fine art, especially the bright geometric patterns of their stylised murals and ceramic designs.

OVERLEAF The golf course at the Lost City is world class, its lush greens and meticulously manicured fairways – entirely out of character with the dry and dusty bushveld that surrounds it – providing a unique oasis in the middle of the Pilanesberg.

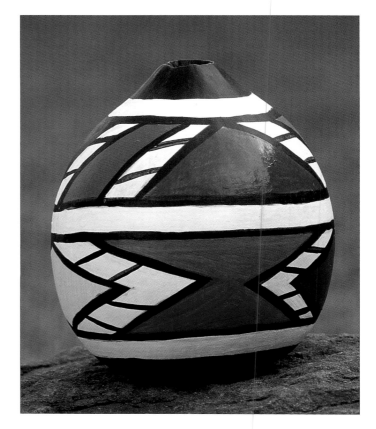

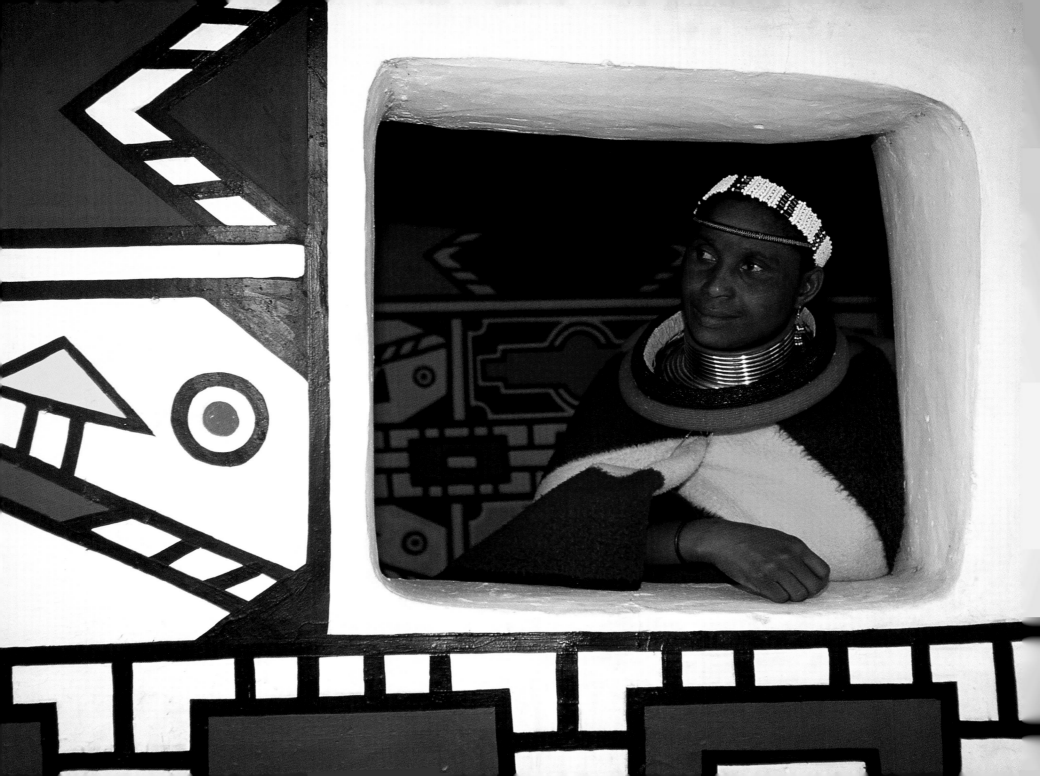

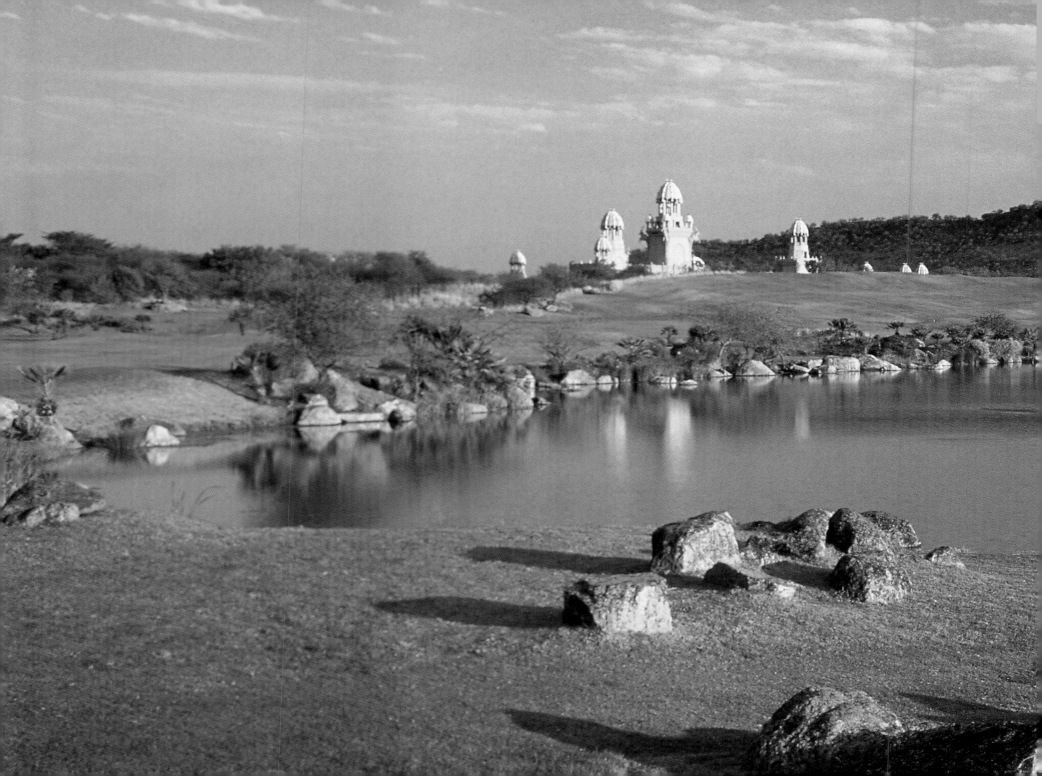

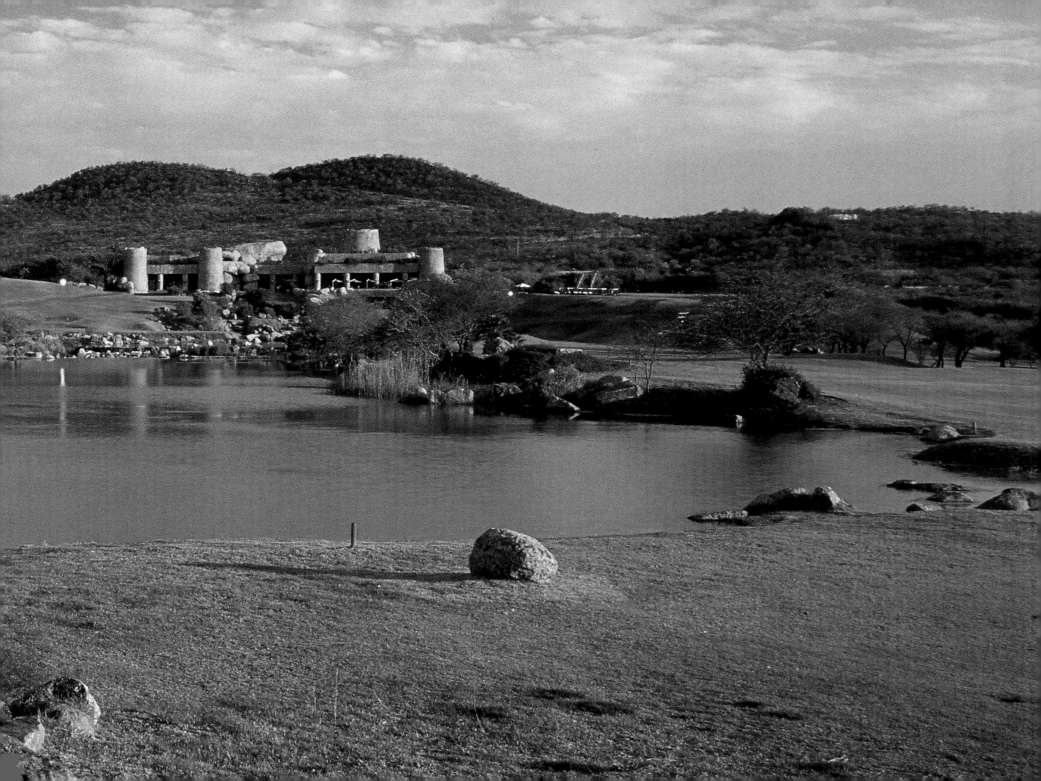

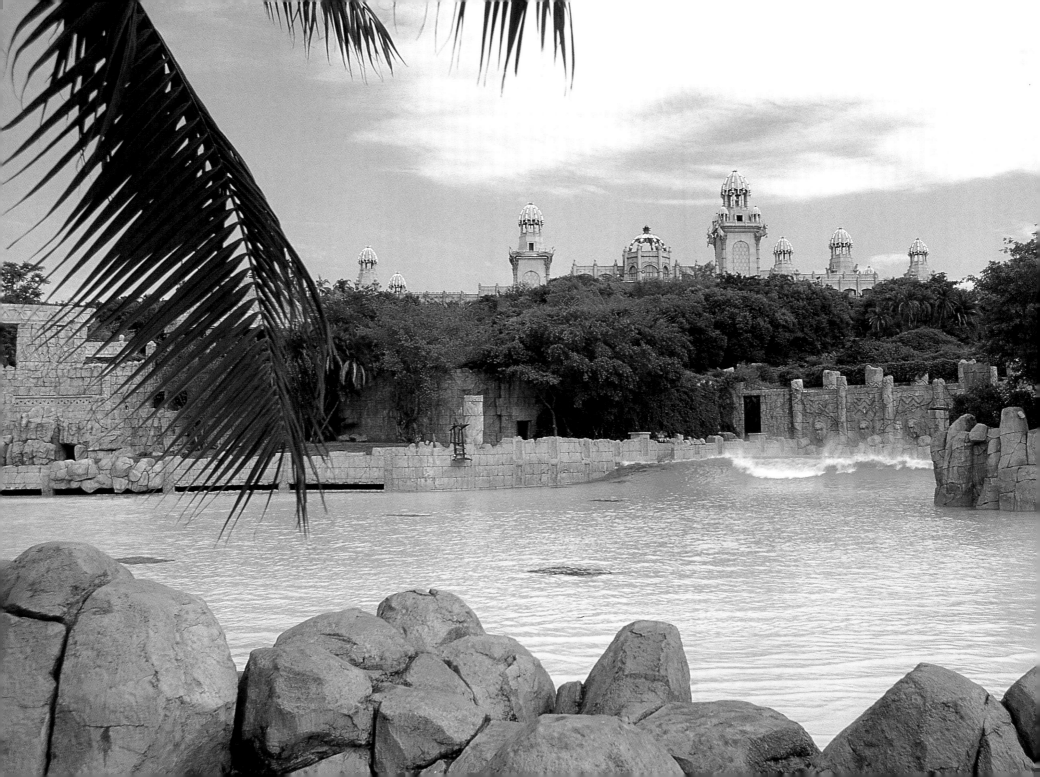

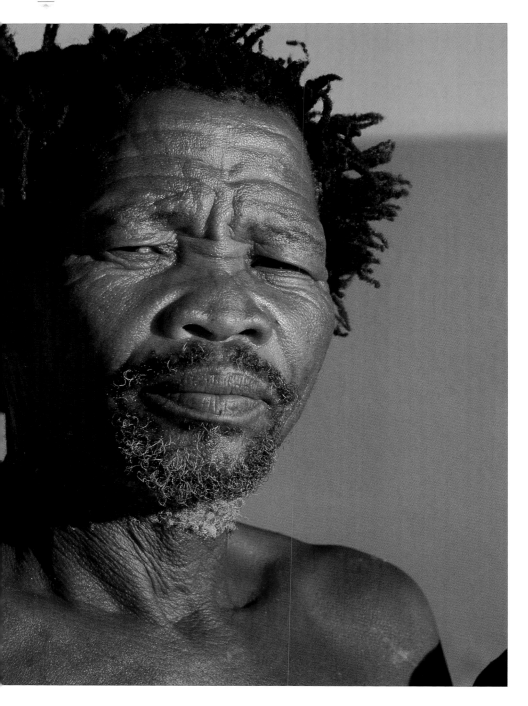

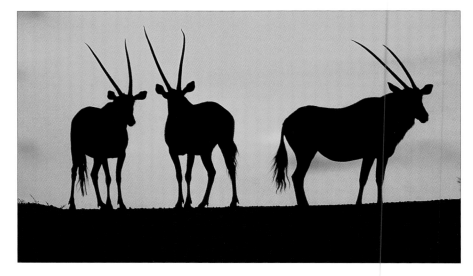

PREVIOUS PAGE, LEFT The grand architecture of The Palace of the Lost City at Sun City is a 'reconstruction' of the seat of a mythical kingdom.

PREVIOUS PAGE, RIGHT The Wave Pool at Sun City recreates the movement of the ocean in the heart of the North West's bushveld.

LEFT AND OPPOSITE Early San hunter-gatherers lived a seminomadic lifestyle, the small family units following the herds of game that crossed their own home territories. These movements coincided with the changes of the seasons and the migrations of prey species. Today, however, the descendants of the San, most of whom rapidly became assimiliated into pastoral groups who moved onto their traditional hunting grounds, lead more Westernised lives, with many having settled into a contemporary village life that allows little opportunity to practise the centuries-old customs and traditions that have been passed down from one generation to the next. Many of the more isolated San communities who have made their home in the desert-like environment of the Kgalagadi in the northern areas of South Africa and southern Botswana, for example, faithfully follow the teachings and ways of their forebears. While some of these communities have adapted in many ways to a more modern lifestyle, traces of their rich and ancient heritage remain an important part of everyday life.

ABOVE Desert-dwelling species, including both animal and plant (such as the numerous succulent varieties that exist in areas such as the Kgalagadi Transfrontier Park, for example), have adapted remarkably well to the dry, desolate and rugged environment. One such mammal species is the oryx, known locally as the gemsbok, which has developed a unique body-cooling system that reduces the temperature of its blood by passing the blood through the nose before it is pumped to the brain.

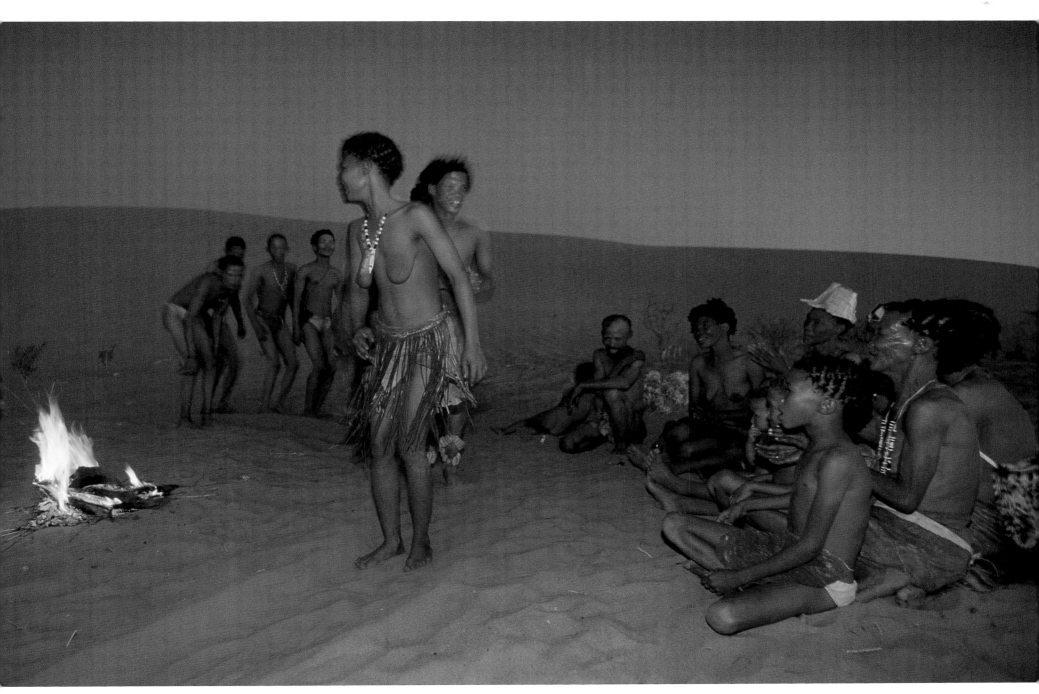

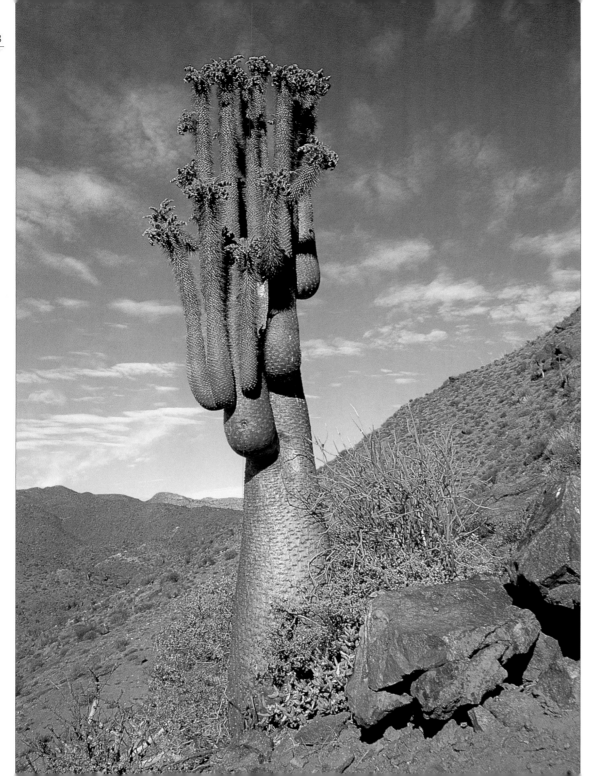

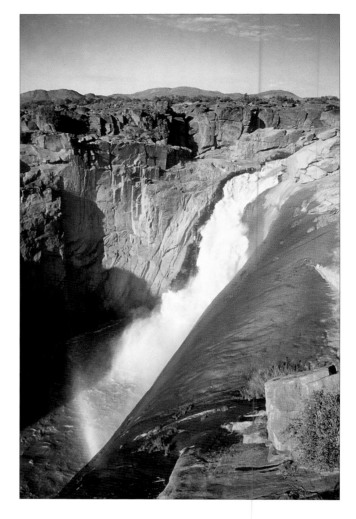

LEFT The vegetation of the stark Richtersveld National Park is sparse and like the peculiarly shaped halfmens (meaning 'part human'), is uniquely adapted to the arid surrounds.

ABOVE The focal point of the Augrabies Falls National Park is the impressive Augrabies Falls, a thunderous torrent of the Orange River that crashes nearly 200 metres (65 feet) into the gorge.

OPPOSITE Many plants in the semidesert of the Northern Cape are endemic, and are able to survive the arid conditions that prevail even along riverbeds, which are more often dry than flowing.

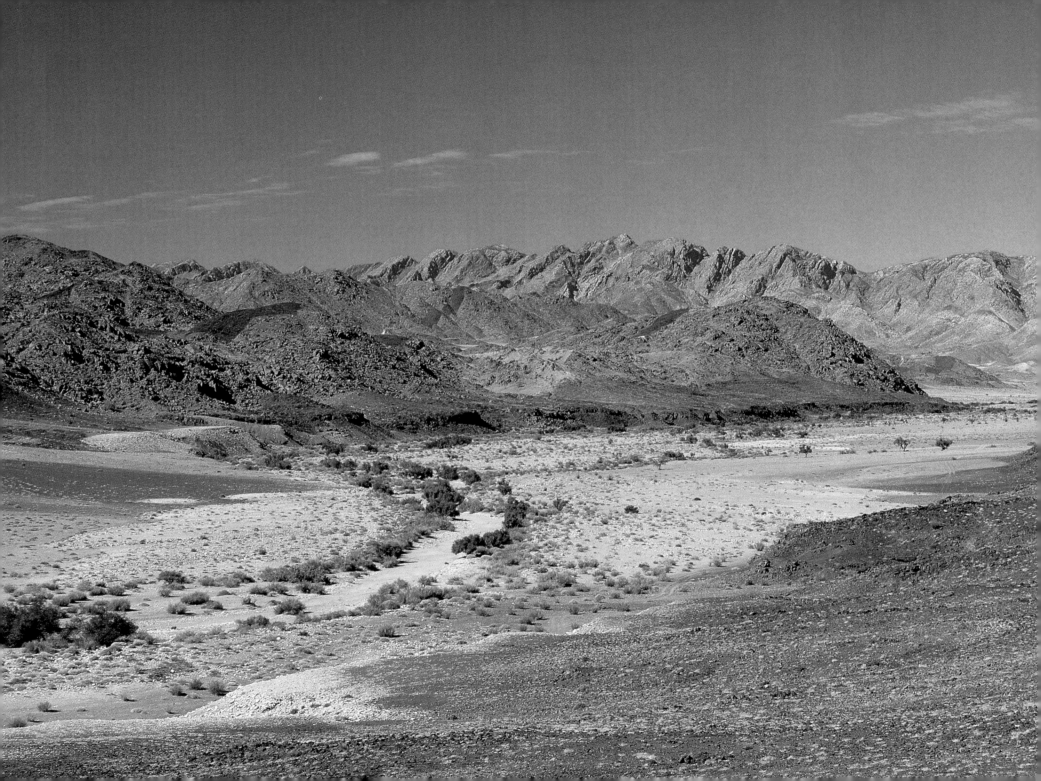

Namibia

Namibia, covering some 824 290 square kilometres (318 260 square miles) of southern Africa's western reaches, consists largely of coastal and desert plain – from the sandy grave of places such as Kolmanskop to the impressive Fish River Canyon and the desolate Skeleton Coast. Like much of the subcontinent, the country has a long history of colonial domination, largely because of the diamonds and other mineral wealth, including uranium, to be found in its soils. And it is precisely the land that remains the nation's most precious asset. Even today, some 200 years since colonists marched into the country and annexed its wealth, the sands of Namibia – particularly the spectacular dunes of the great Namib Desert – have become the prime drawcard for tourists and other intrepid adventurers. The endless red sands of the Namib, comprising rolling dunes dotted only occasionally with meagre vegetation, covers more than a sixth of Namibia's total landmass and, including the beach sands of the famed Skeleton Coast as well as the Namib-Naukluft National Park, consists of approximately 6.5 million hectares

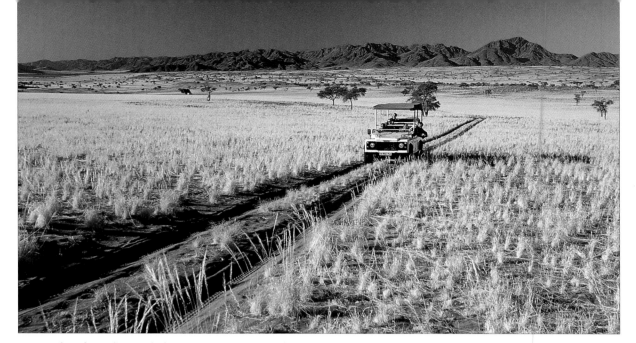

ABOVE The safari industry, which continues to attract significant numbers of overseas visitors, is a mainstay of the Namibian economy and provides an important source of income for many locals. The NabibRand Nature Reserve is a favourite.

(16 million acres). But while the expanse of sand and gravel, tucked haphazardly between towering dunes, is dry and – for the most part – quite literally deserted, it hosts a phenomenal number of both flora (most famously, the indigenous welwitschia, which grows nowhere else in the world) and fauna that have specifically adapted over the centuries to life in one of Africa's least accommodating deserts. In fact, about 200 vertebrates are endemic to the region; herds of gemsbok (oryx) roam the sands, there is an impressive bird population, a number of succulent plant varieties, thousands of insect species and more than 20 reptiles.

Straddling Namibia's western shore are silvery beach sands that stretch from the Namib-Naukluft National Park in the country's southern extremities to the country's northern border. This is the Skeleton Coast, 1.6 million hectares (4 million acres) sandwiched between the arid interior in the east and the cold waters of the Atlantic in the west. The landscape here, although eerily empty of the conspicuous

wildlife so typical in the rest of southern Africa, is surprisingly rich in a wildlife of its own, scattered across two rather distinct regions. Unfortunately, travellers are not

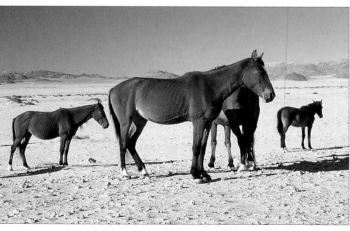

ABOVE The Namib is today perhaps just as well known for its roaming herd of wild horses as it is for its indigenous wildlife.

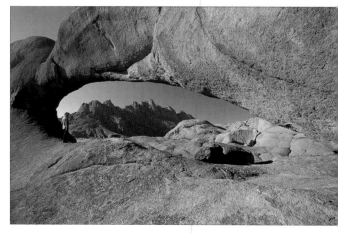

ABOVE The granite domes and peaks of the Spitzkoppe near Usakos stand 700 metres (2 296 feet) over the arid surrounds.

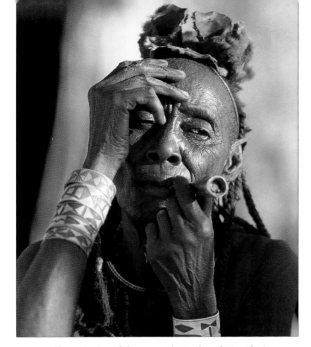

ABOVE *The majority of the pastoral Himba of Namibia's northwest continue to follow the traditions of their forefathers.*

permitted entry, and will probably miss out on one of the great spectacles on offer – the unique strandwolf wandering an empty beach. The Skeleton Coast National Park is an untamed wilderness divided into two main regions: dry gravel plains interrupted by seasonal river waters in the south and the baking Namib in the north. This is a region, however, that sees great volatility when it comes to nature's elements, beaten relentlessly by wind and the action of the ocean. While relatively few mammal species are to be found here, the Skeleton Coast National Park is known for its birds, such as cormorants, avocets, pelicans and even flamingoes.

Despite the fact that the vegetation in Namibia is meagre and water very scarce indeed, the country's tourism industry has seen a considerable upturn in recent years, most especially since it gained independence. This has, of course, also meant that the all-important components of its vast natural heritage have become one of the nation's most significant income earners. Today, parks such as the Namib-

Naukluft, Etosha – at 22 270 square kilometres (8 598 square miles), the country's most prominent reserve – and a variety of smaller but equally important wildlife sanctuaries have become vital to the wellbeing of not only the land as a whole, but specifically the national economy.

While still considered small and not as well developed as other southern African capitals, Windhoek remains a very popular stop on Namibia's tourist trail. The mood here is truly African: the sunsets are indeed golden, the horizons endless and the immediate environment alive with the potential for adventure. Windhoek is the economic heart of Namibia, with a total population of about 1.7 million, about half of whom are Ovambo and the remaining half comprising Kavango, Herero, Damara, Himba and white Namibians. The city is a popular tourist centre, awash with

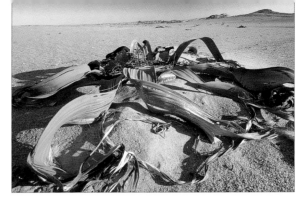

ABOVE *The welwitschia, which only bears two leaves, is indigenous to the Namib, with many specimens 500 years old.*

colour and alive with the sounds of its people. Facilities are more than adequate and the infrastructure of the latter-day city surprisingly well geared towards the international traveller. As such, the capital is the real gateway to the adventures on offer on the coast and in the desert and beyond.

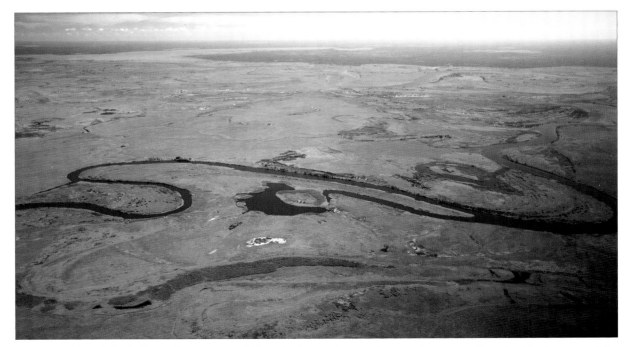

ABOVE *East Caprivi, in the far northeastern parts of Namibia, is a richly watered expanse that is virtually enclosed by the waters of the Chobe, Linyanti and Kwando rivers.*

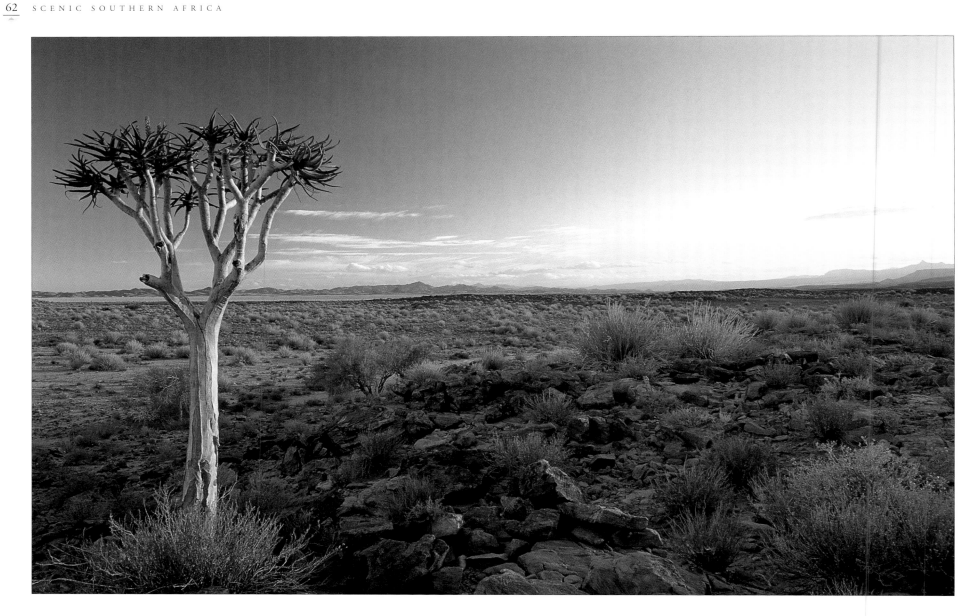

<small>ABOVE</small> Although Namibia's Fish River Canyon does not boast a great diversity of vegetation, the quiver tree is typical, and it is from the bark of this tree that San hunters crafted their quivers.

<small>OPPOSITE</small> The Fish River Canyon, gouged from rock by the river water, is the second largest in the world.

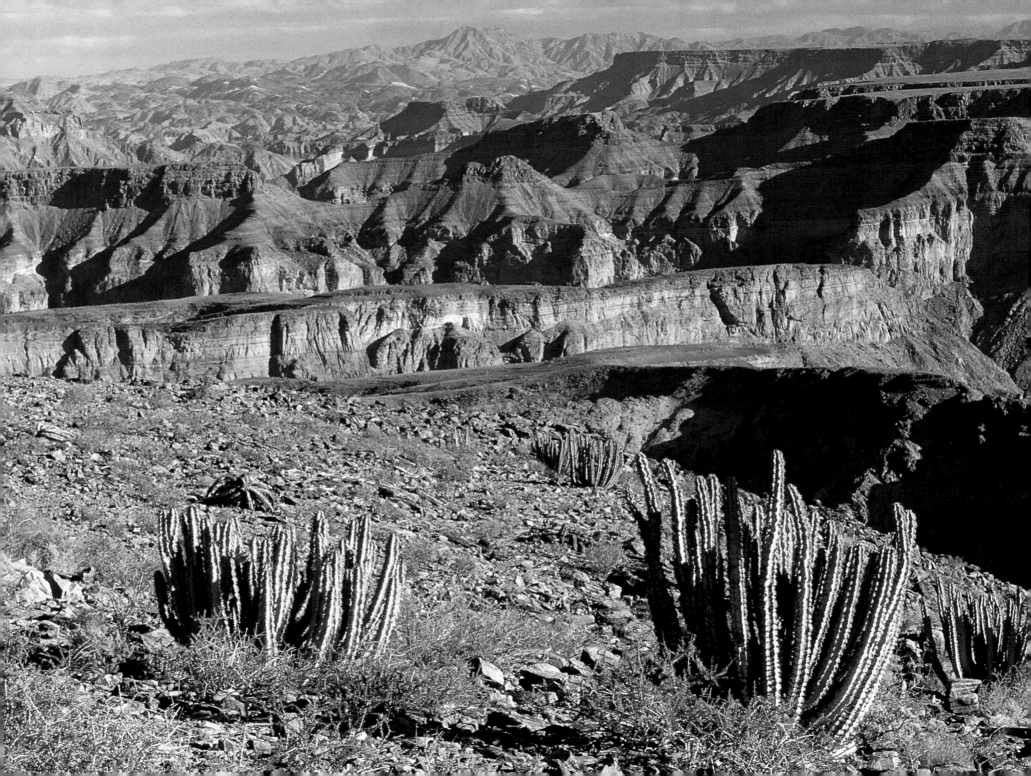

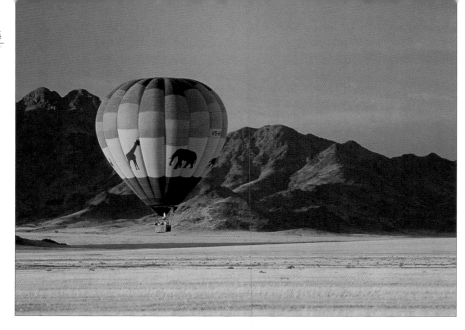

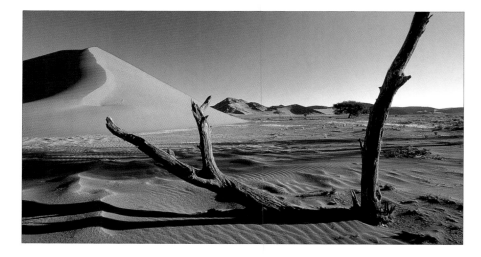

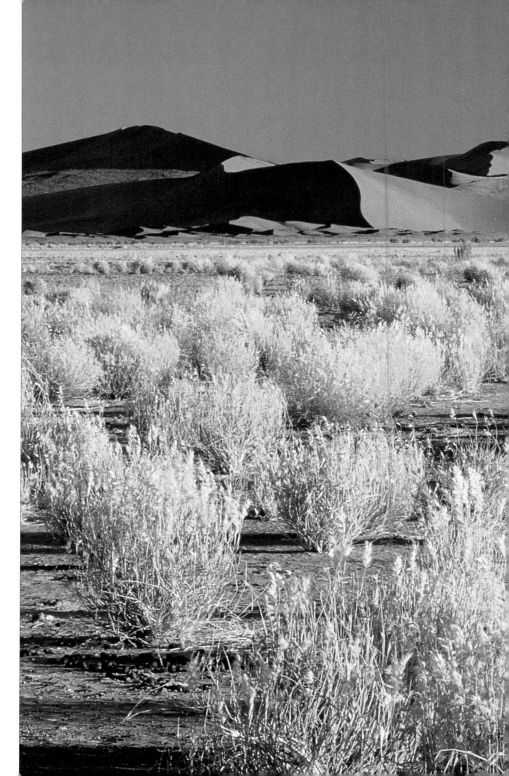

TOP Ballooning, which offers breathtaking aerial views over the Namib, takes advantage of the atmospheric pockets of hot air typical of desert conditions.

ABOVE The dune landscape of areas such as Sossusvlei are fairly typical of much of the Namib Desert, but may vary greatly in the density of vegetative cover.

OPPOSITE Although the romantic notion of the Namib dictates uninterrupted expanses of blood-red sand dune, vast stretches do indeed feature shrubs and grasses typical of the region.

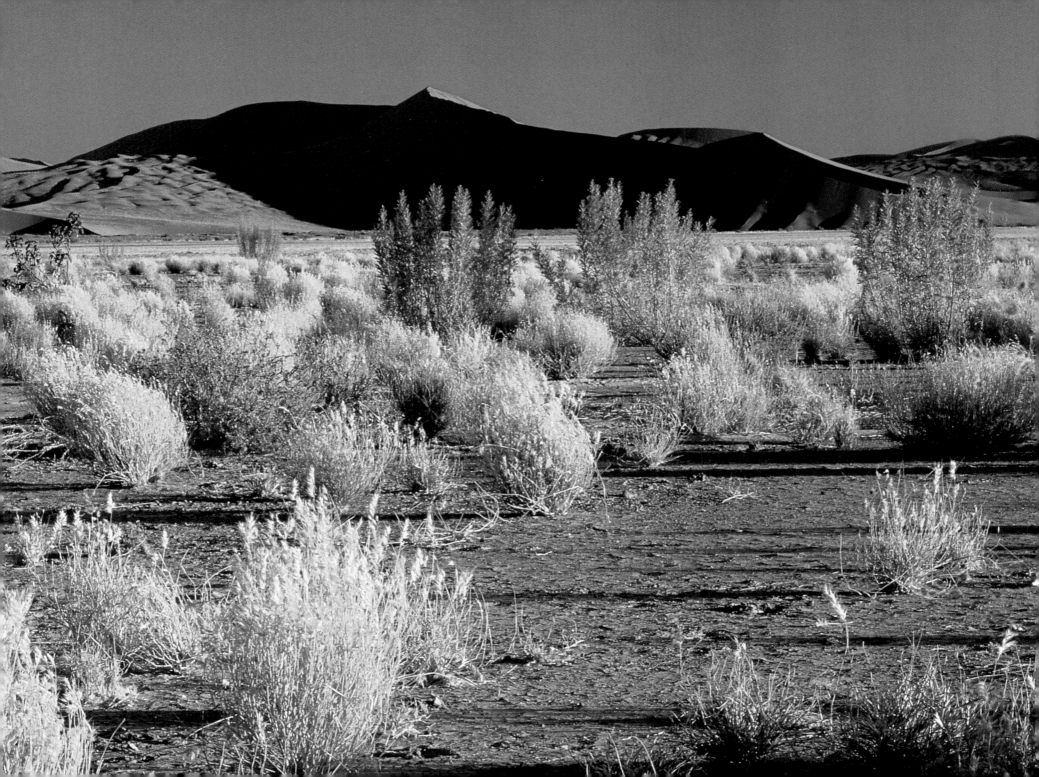

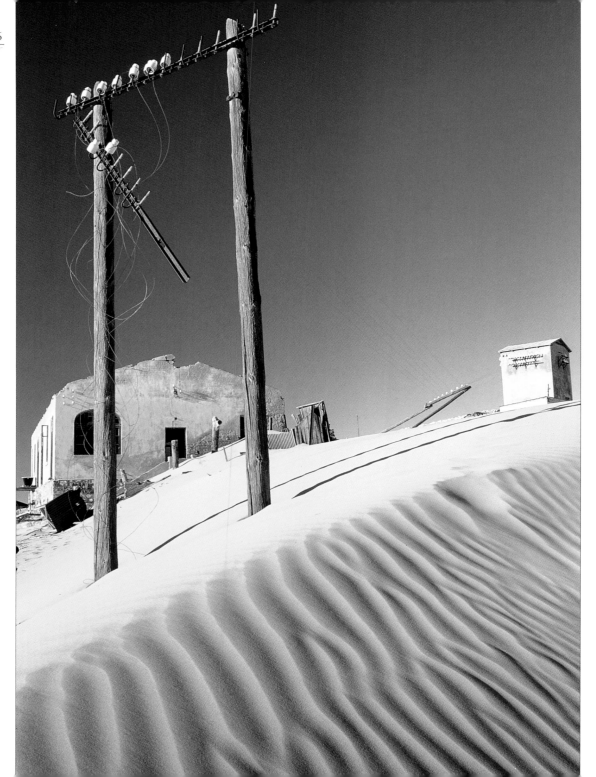

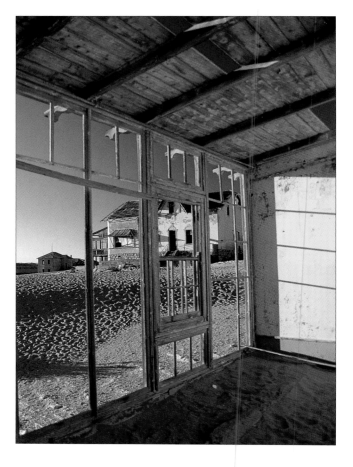

Left Even though the harsh conditions of the Namib may seem unsuited to human habitation, die-hard prospectors at Kolmanskop near Lüderitz, for example, battled the elements in their determination to find their fortune in diamonds in the early 1900s. Above When equally promising finds were unearthed around Oranjemund, places such as Kolmanskop were rapidly deserted for better prospects. Today all that remains are ruins of the once grand homes, rapidly being swallowed up by the encroaching desert sands. Opposite From the air, the structure of the sand dunes appear to be a permanent aspect of the environment. In many parts of the Namib, however, both the sands and the dunes they create tend to shift regularly, seldom remaining static for very long.

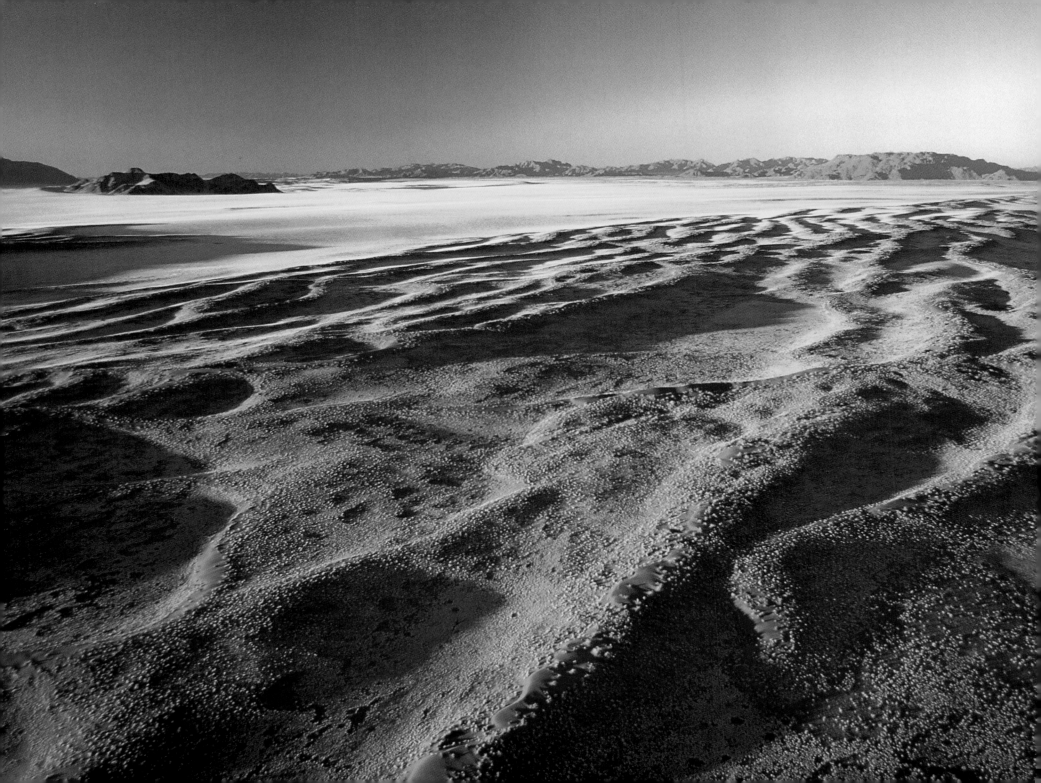

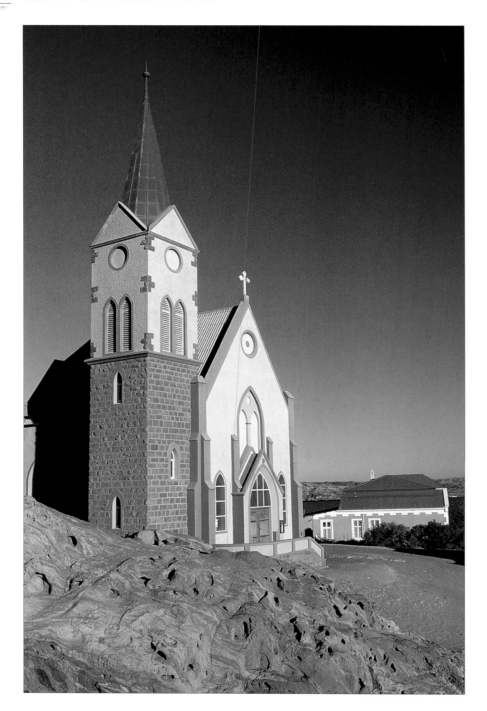

LEFT AND BELOW Many of the towns and villages, such as Lüderitz, that lay scattered across Namibia, most especially along its apparently endless coastline, originated with the settlement of colonists such as the Germans who made their home here, particularly in the days of the 'diamond rush'. The German settlers, including many missionaries determined to convert locals to Christianity, erected churches, schools and a number of administrative buildings that continue to bear testimony to the European culture.

OPPOSITE Today, much of the colonial heritage of places such as Lüderitz remains intact, with both the architecture and the language of the German settlers contributing enormously to the local character. Even after Namibian independence in the 1980s, the colonial names bestowed on places such as Lüderitz, Swakopmund and Mariental remain.

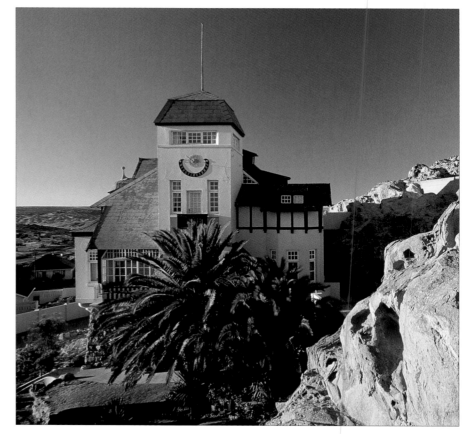

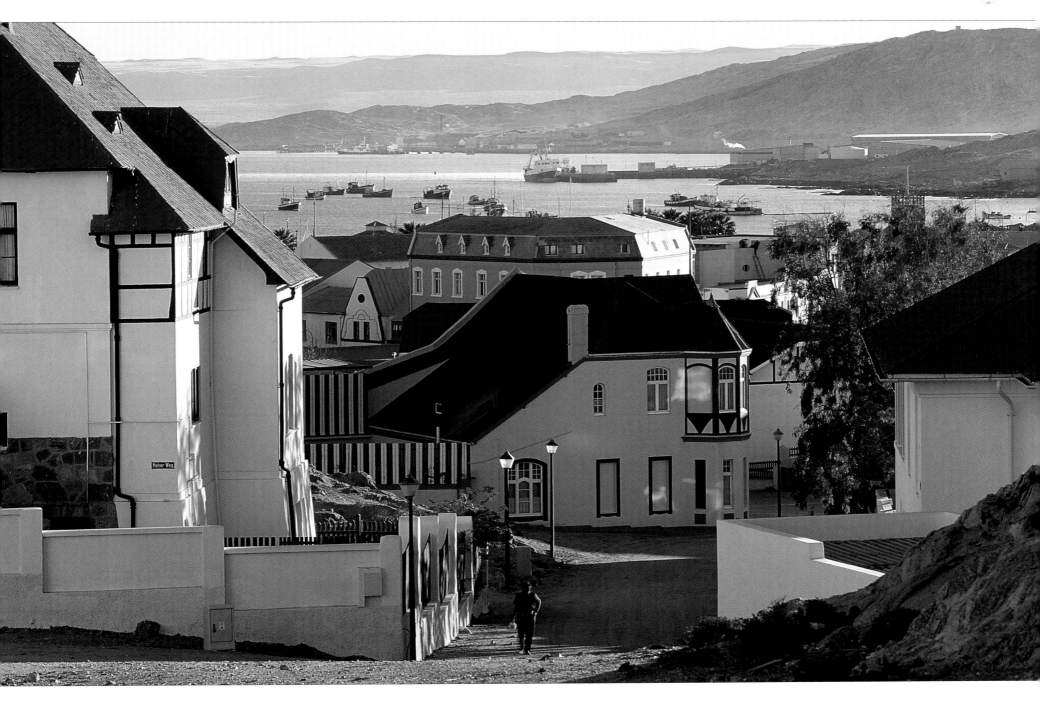

BELOW The Namib is indeed a living desert, with small creatures such as the webfooted gecko commonplace on the dune landscape.

BOTTOM The *Stenocara eburnea* desert beetle feeds on detritus in the sand.

RIGHT Situated at the southernmost point of the shoreline known as the Skeleton Coast, the otherwise dry Swakopmund sees its fair share of coastal fog.

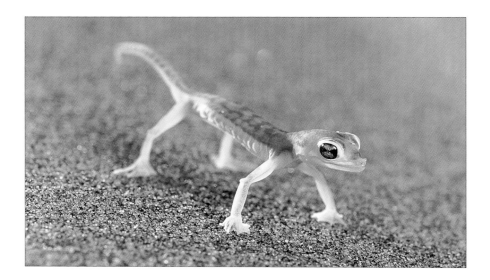

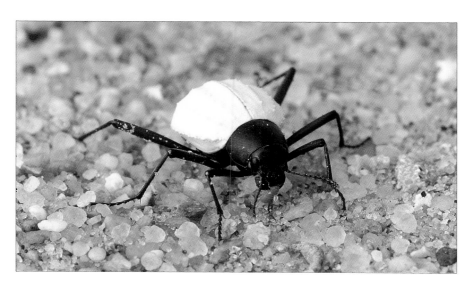

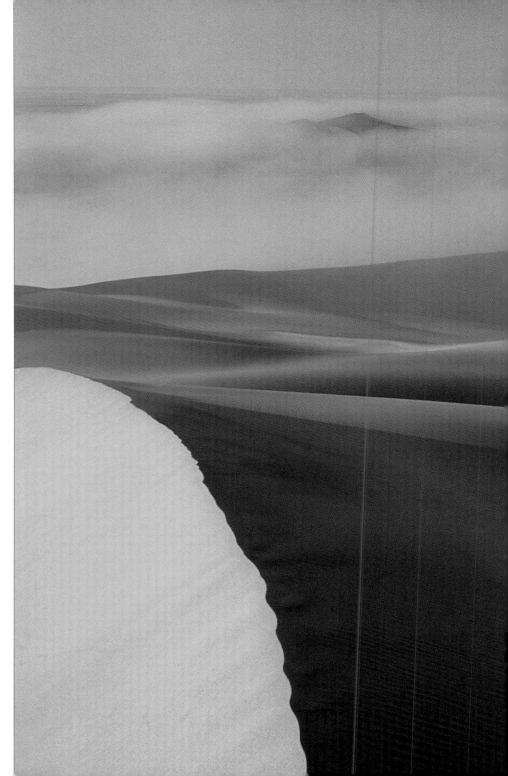

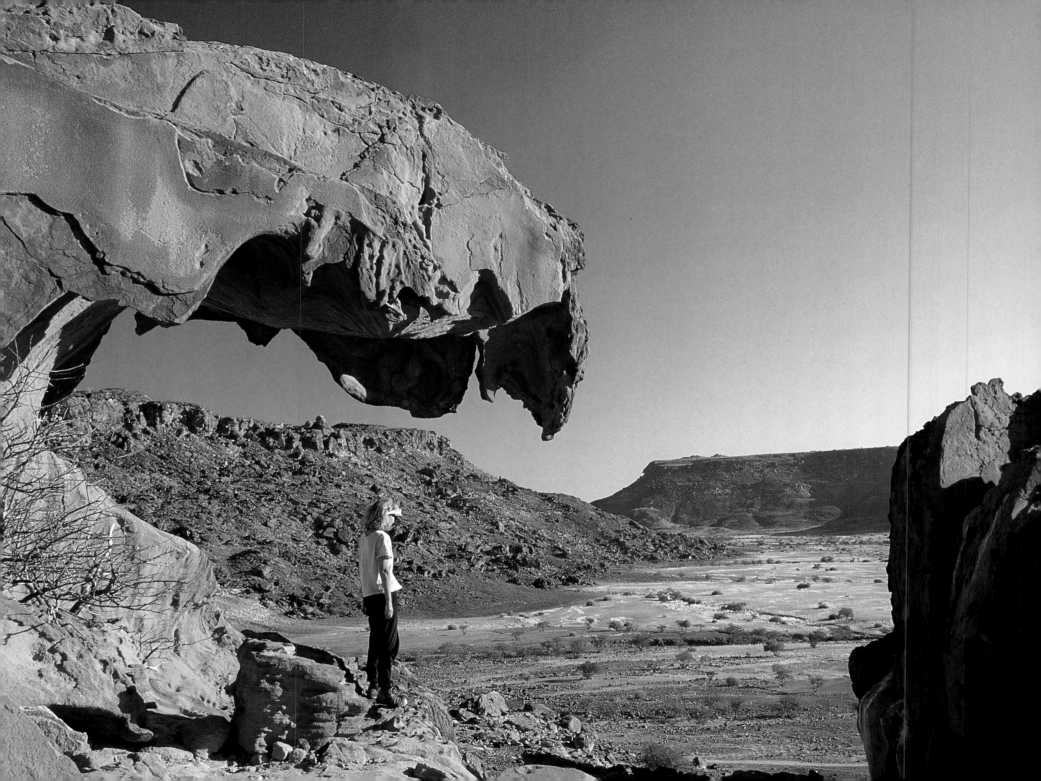

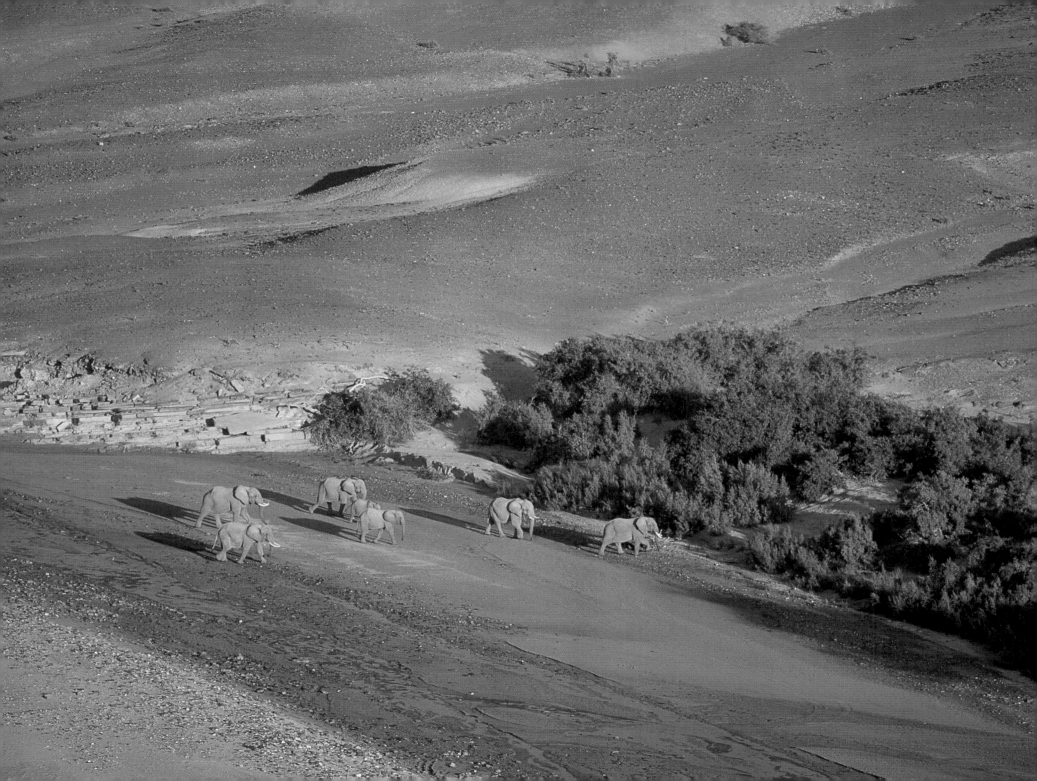

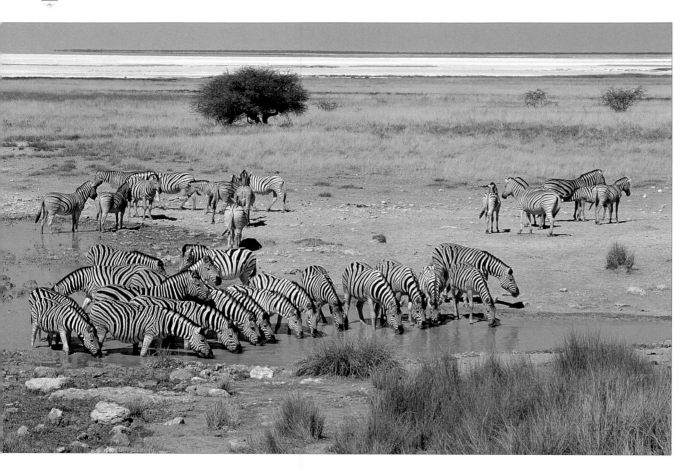

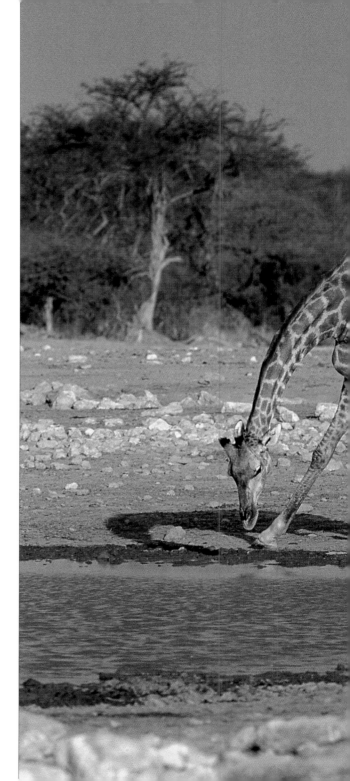

PREVIOUS PAGE, LEFT The rock formations of Twyfelfontein in the Korixas region provide a showcase for some of the world's most impressive rock engravings. This open-air gallery boasts a wealth of indigenous art, including more than 2 400 petroglyphs – of local wildife such as elephant, lion and rhino – said to have been engraved into the hard rock some 5 000 years ago.

PREVIOUS PAGE, RIGHT The desert-dwelling elephants of Kaokaland and Damaraland, shown here crossing the Hoarusib River near Purros, have adopted a unique way of life on the desert sand. These 50-plus individuals are able to do without regular water, and can go as long as four to five days without drinking, travelling more than 50 kilometres (31 miles) in a single day in order to reach isolated water holes and drinking areas.

TOP Namibia's wildlife, such as these Burchell's zebra at Etosha, depends entirely on the forces of nature. When the rains fall in the summer months, water may be plentiful, but in the dry winter water is pitifully scarce.

RIGHT Etosha National Park was once an enormous lake. Today, wildlife such as impala and giraffe, survive on the seasonal waters of the remaining pans, which fill briefly with water during the rains. Wildlife tend to migrate from one small water source to the next as supplies evaporate during the dry spells, when water holes revert to being little more than dustbowls.

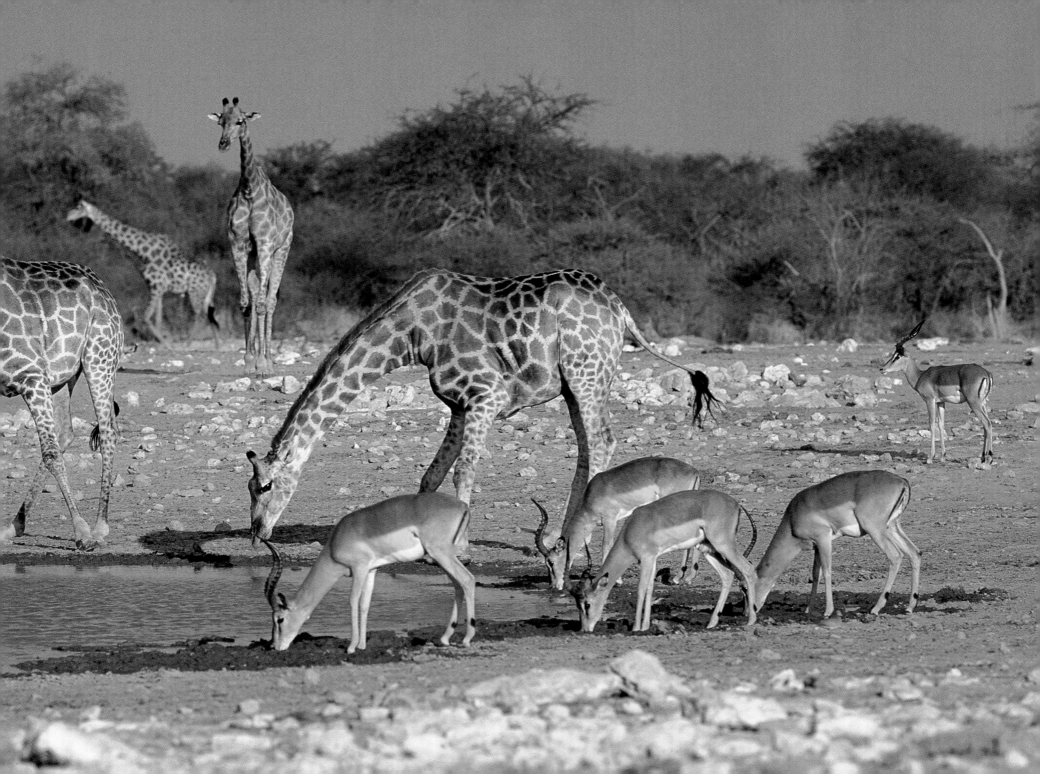

Botswana

With no less than 18 per cent of Botswana devoted to national parks and other conservation efforts such as those that centre around the spectacular Okavango Delta and smaller, private reserves, the country's conservation record is, in many ways, an impressive one, particularly when it comes to the management of its wildlife, spread across the 581 730 square kilometres (224 600 square miles) of its total landcover. This, of course, has resulted in equally impressive development in Botswana's tourism industry and today Botswana's top game reserves – such as Moremi and Chobe – are internationally acclaimed as some of Africa's most significant. As a result, Botswana's faunal heritage is now one of the country's most lucrative, accounting for just over 40 per cent of the nation's formal employment sector and bringing no less than US$50 million a year into the local economy. But the most important aspect of this ever-growing, capital-inducing development is ecotourism, a trend that has quickly usurped Botswana's hunting industry as one of its top earners of foreign exchange. It follows that

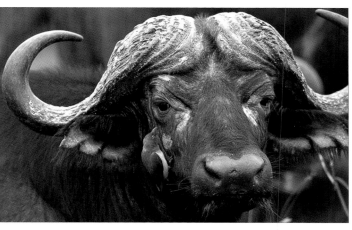

ABOVE *Botswana's wildlife heritage is one of the most spectacular in Africa, boasting all of the Big Five, including the buffalo.*

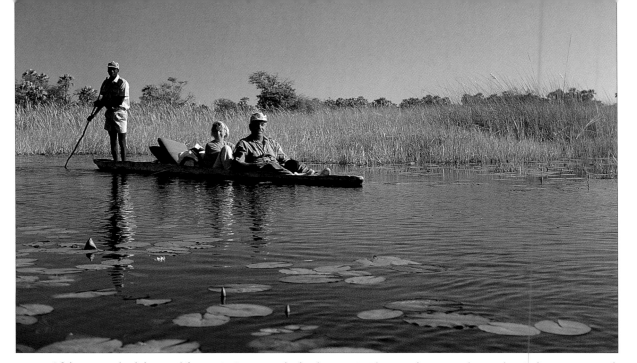

ABOVE *Of the many splendid natural features in Botswana, by far the most significant and most popular are the winding waterways of the Okavango Delta, to which visitors flock in order to take traditional* mokoro *rides.*

Botswana has accepted a praiseworthy compromise on policies of land usage. Today, it is one of the leading ecotourism destinations on the continent – and certainly the subcontinent – specialising in relatively small, exclusive groups of moneyed travellers determined to experience the very best of the local excursions, such as the popular elephant-back safaris and leisurely *mokoro* trips along the Okavango Delta's winding waterways.

Much of the Botswana landscape is dry and sparsely vegetated – most notable is the wind-blown Kalahari – and yet it is host to a great many of southern Africa's landmark natural features, including the water wonderland of the Okavango Delta, which stretches some 15 000 square kilometres (5 800 square miles) when in flood. It is, however, precisely the combination of these diverse environments, spectacularly rich in game and bird species, that are the great attraction to so many visitors. The delta, for instance,

comprises a far-reaching web of nutrient-rich lagoons and channels that play host to thriving populations of hippo and buffalo, crocodiles and antelope such as the exceptionally well-adapted sitatunga and lechwe resident in the marshlands. But while the Okavango constitutes the popular image of wild Botswana at its most spectacular, the Moremi Game Reserve on the delta's eastern border comprises 2 000 square kilometres (770 square miles) of stark bushland punctuated with mopane woodland as well as both lagoon and floodplain. Naturally, it boasts many of the big game that have earned the region its enviable reputation: sightings of elephant, buffalo, leopard, lion, cheetah and a number of antelope species are commonplace. Much the same is true of Chobe National Park, a wilderness of 10 000 square kilometres (3 800 square miles) demarcated by the massive Linyanti-Chobe river system and home to some 35 000 elephant and more than 450 bird species.

Not the same is true, of course, of the great Kalahari, which makes up more than 80 per cent of Botswana. Scorched by a baking sun for much of the year, this vast stretch of sand between the Orange River in the south and the equatorial regions to the north is either lashed by dust and sand or seasonal summer rains. The Kalahari is said to have been formed about 200 million years ago when the Gondwana supercontinent started to disintegrate to form the landmasses that today make up the southern hemisphere. The mineral deposits that form its foundation today are, however, some 300 million years old, and some of the rock formations that have become so much a landmark of the region may even be three billion years old.

In contrast to its vast wildernesses, the Botswanan capital, Gaborone, is a rather small city, but it has never-

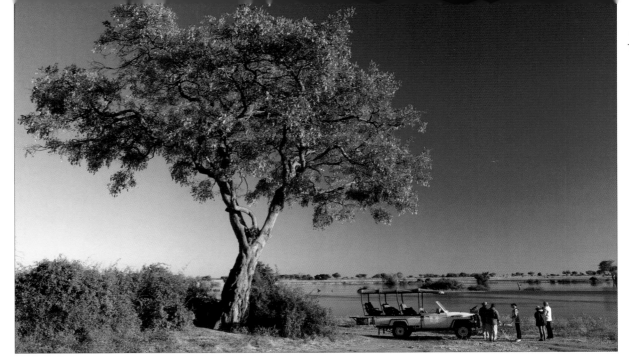

ABOVE *The tourism industry thrives in Botswana, the most popular excursions including safaris along the course of the Chobe, one of the country's most important rivers.*

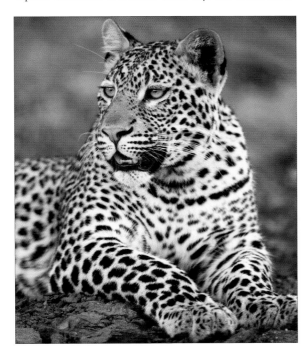

ABOVE *Leopards are prized in the Mashatu Game Reserve.*
RIGHT *The African fish eagle is Botswana's most conspicuous.*

theless seen remarkable development since it was first pronounced the nation's capital in the 1960s. Gaborone is considered very laidback when it comes to capital cities – even by African standards – but because it has great mineral wealth, it is considered one of the subregion's most significant urban centres. The road network lends the capital a somewhat cosmopolitan air, its modern face accommodating an impressive number of first-class hotels and restaurants, while at the same time embracing its indigenous African heritage. In fact, with both Khutse and Mokolodi so nearby, it is one of the few cities in the world with wildlife reserves on its urban perimeter.

About 3 per cent of the population comprises the San peoples, who once thrived on the extensive tracts of near-desert land across the central regions of southern Africa. While a large number of the descendants of these peoples remain within the political boundaries of modern-day

Botswana, smaller communities are confined to arid corners of the Kalahari in South Africa and Namibia. It is thought that San hunter-gatherers originated about 10 000 years ago but relatively little remains of the ancient traditions.

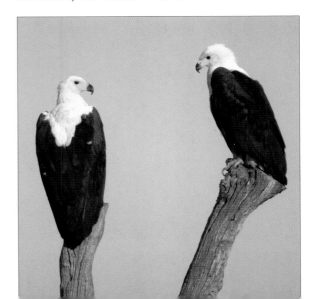

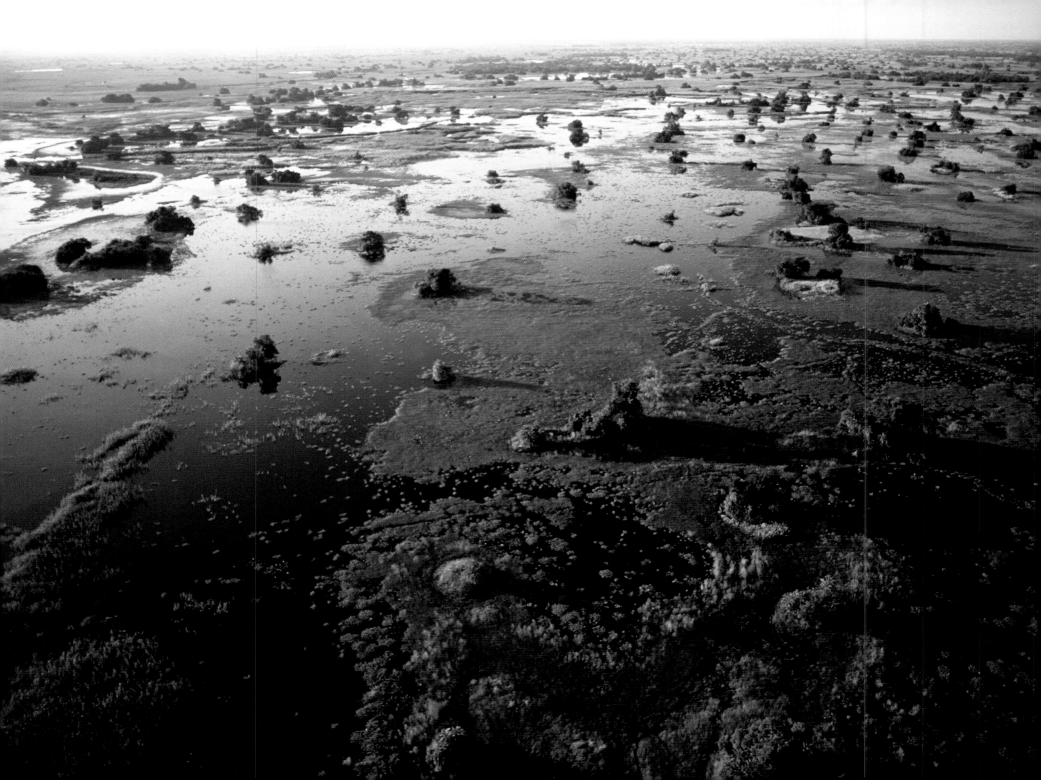

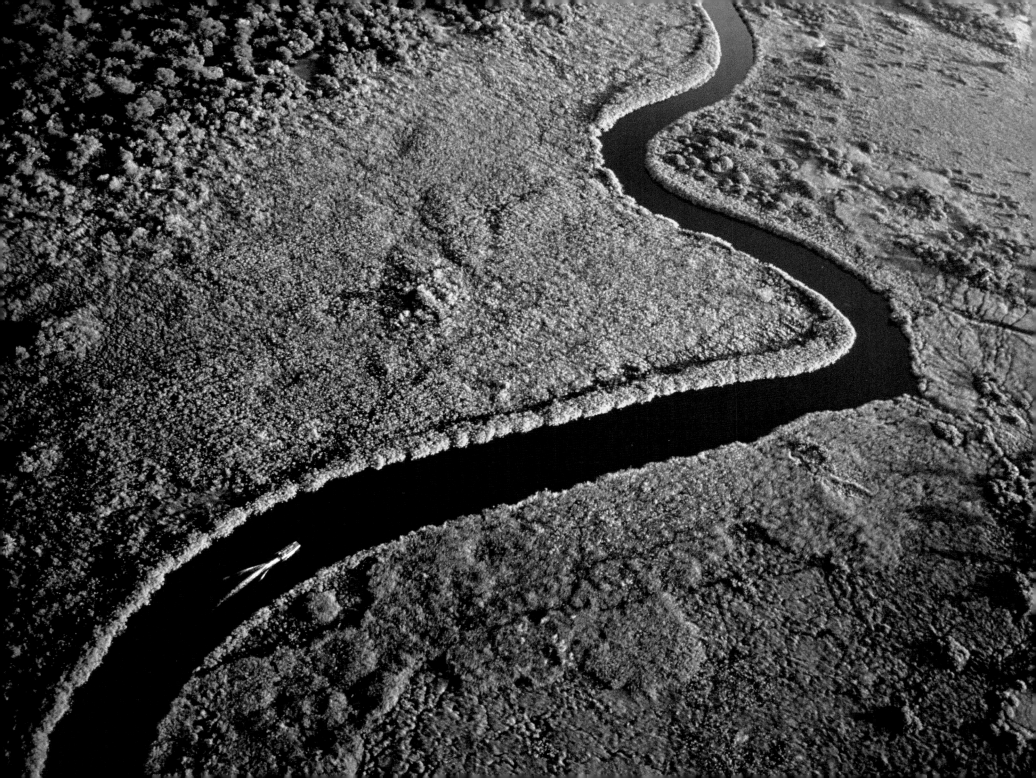

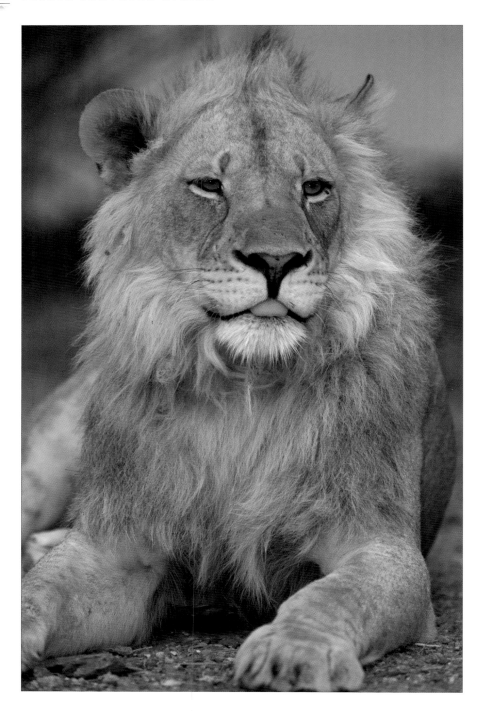

PREVIOUS PAGE, LEFT The Okavango Delta is a complex network of permanent floodplains that are home not only to an extraordinary diversity of plant life that has specifically adapted to the watery surrounds, but also an astounding number of mammal species that rely on the abundant waters of these magnificent wetlands.

PREVIOUS PAGE, RIGHT Because the Okavango Delta and its Panhandle make up one of the country's – if not the continent's – most significant landmarks and is one of the most popular tourist drawcards, it sees a fair amount of tourist traffic, although conservation officials are careful to limit waterbound transport.

LEFT AND OPPOSITE The Northern Tuli Game Reserve – home to the lion and many other big-game species – is one of the country's most out-of-the-way wildlife sanctuaries, and because it does not see as many annual visitors as its more popular counterparts, it remains entirely unspoilt.

BELOW The landscape of Chobe National Park varies from swamp and grassland to flood-plain and bushveld, bordered in the north by the massive Linyanti-Chobe river system, a wilderness that remains the life force for an endless parade of wildlife, including a great variety of birdlife and antelope species such as the lechwe.

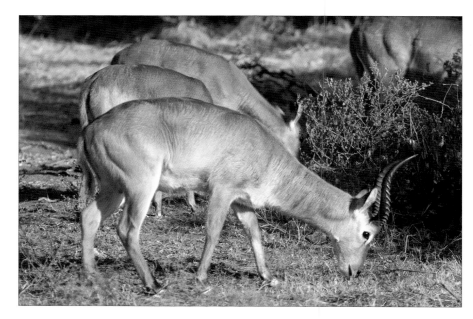

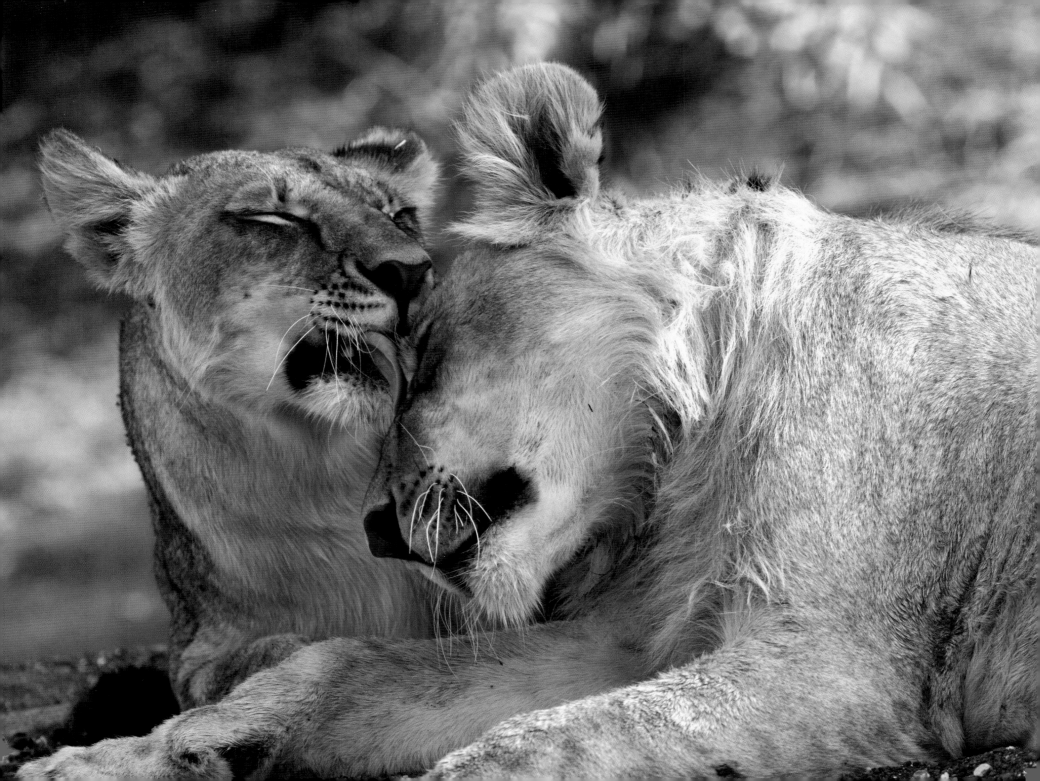

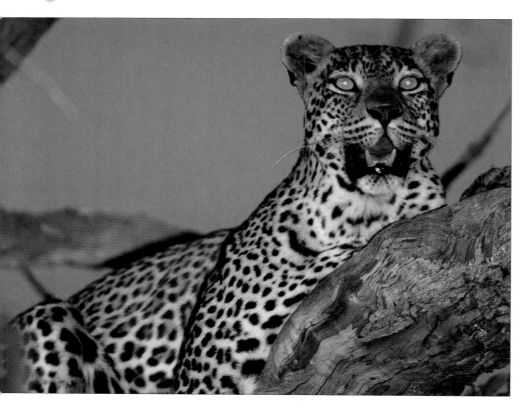

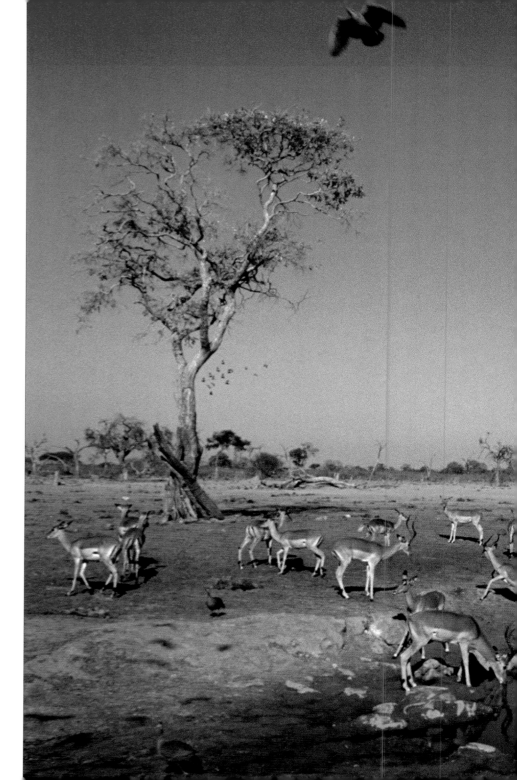

ABOVE With the establishment of Botswana's tourism industry, conservation areas such as the country's national parks have been added to with the development of a number of private reserves and sanctuaries. Prime among these is the Mashatu Game Reserve in Tuli, with its prized leopard population.

RIGHT Savuti, visited here by a herd of impala, as well as guineafowl and sandgrouse, lies at the very heart of Chobe National Park and visitors making their way to this rather inaccessible region are compelled to do so in four-wheel-drive vehicles. However, because it is reached with some difficulty, the rewards are great indeed and Chobe's Savuti Camp is blessed with many memorable wildlife sightings.

OVERLEAF While Chobe National Park is renowned for the diversity of its wildlife, it is the 70 000-plus elephant population that parades along the river front that is the enduring face of the great river. These mammoth beasts are the prime attraction, and the national park and surrounding lodges offer river trips such as the ever-popular 'booze cruises' that take visitors as close to the drinking elephants as possible.

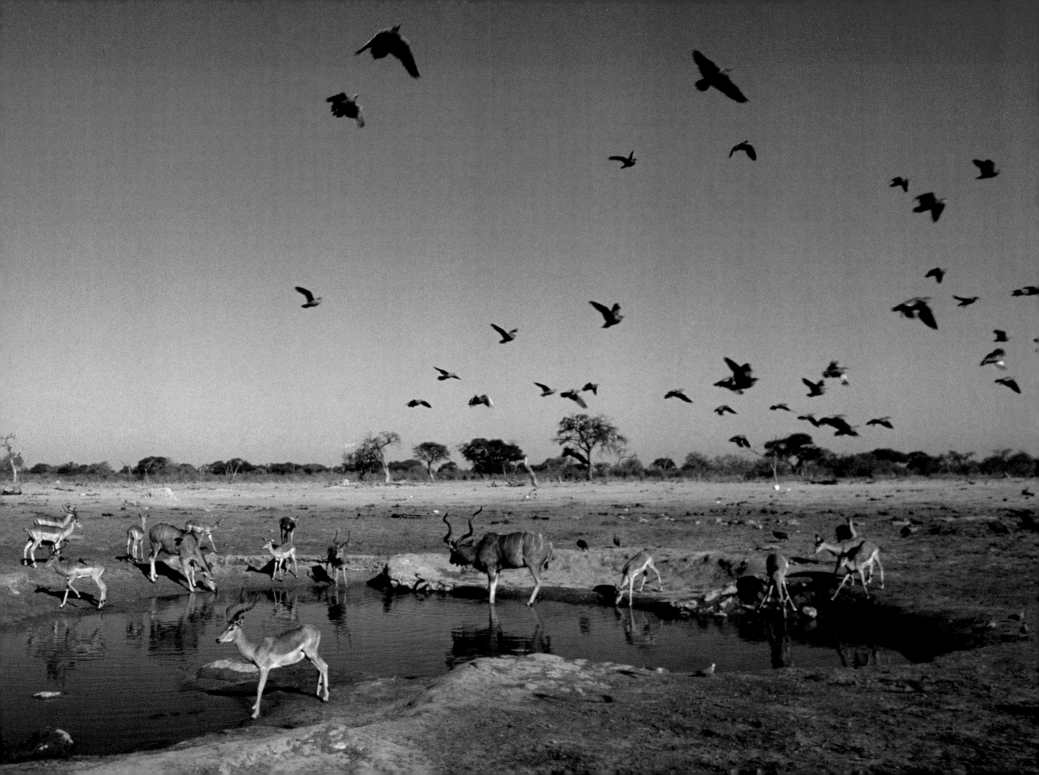

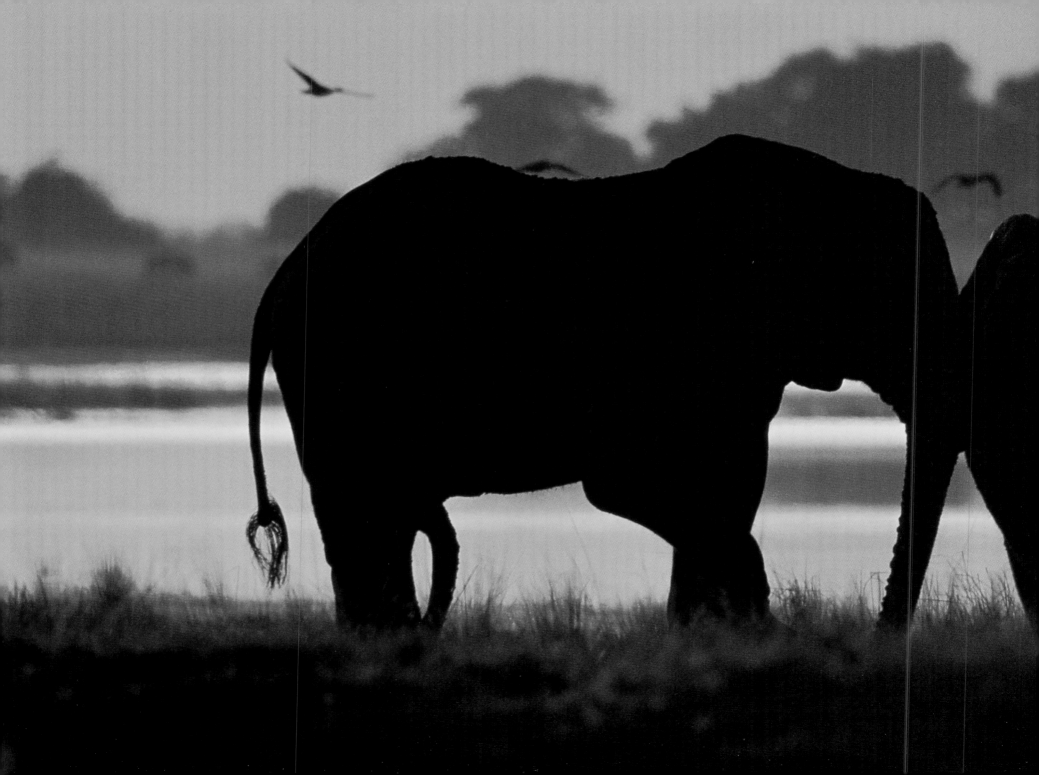

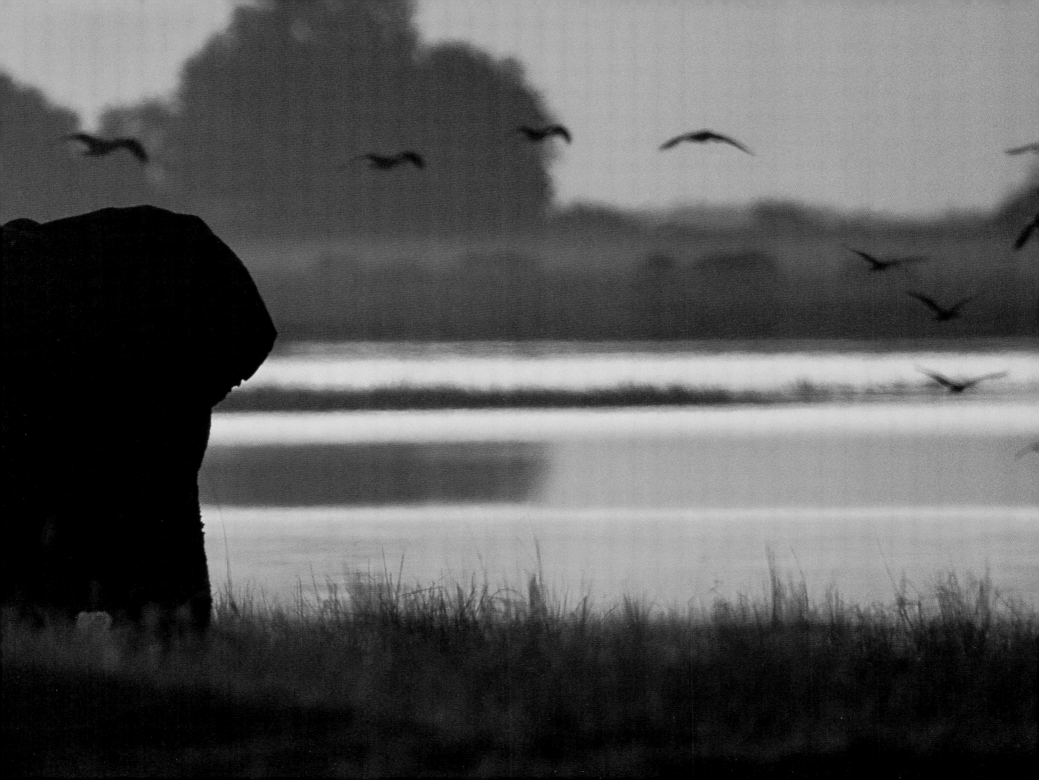

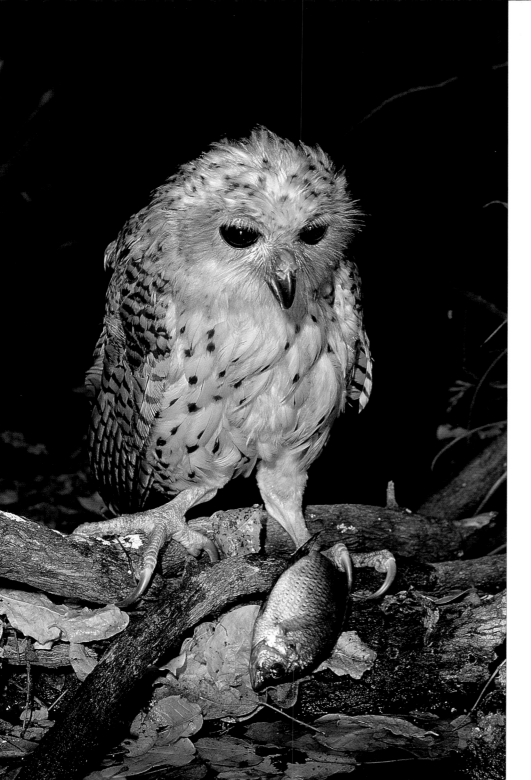

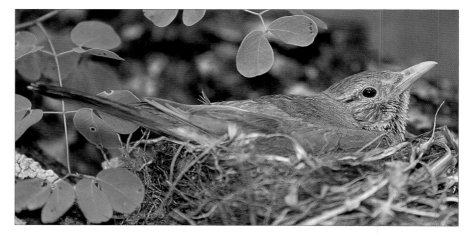

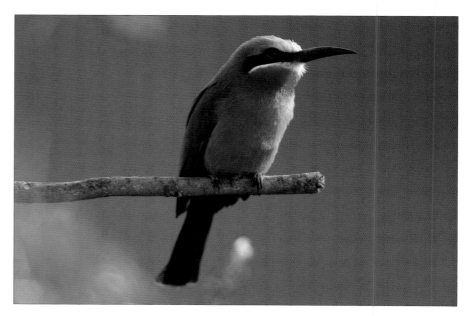

LEFT Just as much as Botswana is known for the enormous diversity of its mammal life, its avifaunal variety is equally impressive, with many of the species thriving specifically along the country's many water courses. The Pel's fishing owl, for example, may be spotted around the slow-moving rivers.

TOP The Kurrichane thrush is a common inhabitant of thornveld and woodland areas.

ABOVE The whitefronted bee-eater is frequently encountered along steep riverbanks.

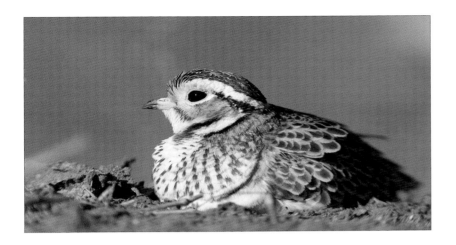

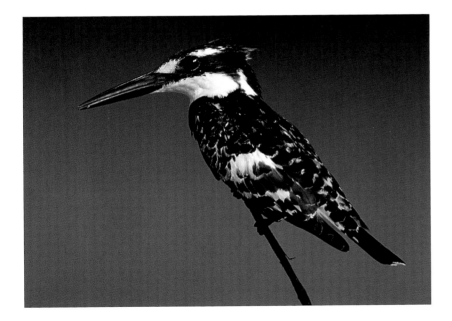

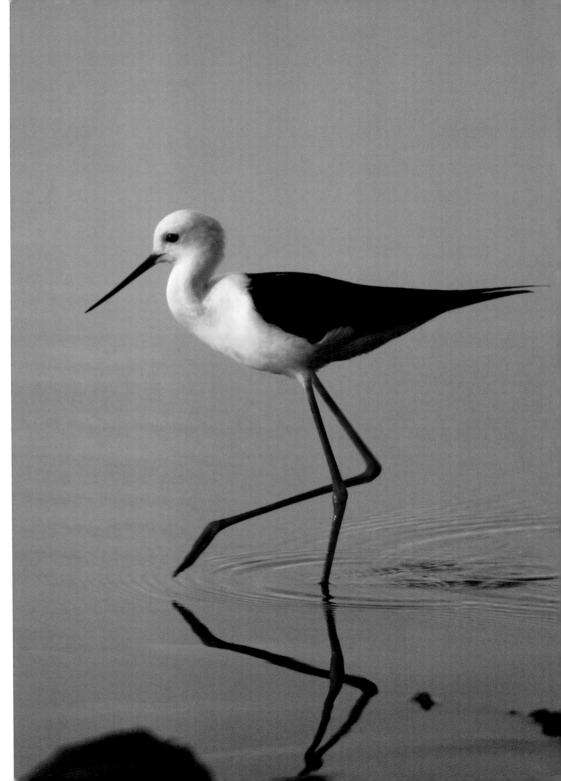

TOP Although many bird species tend to frequent water sources, just as many have adapted well to the large parts of Botswana that are considerably less hospitable. One such species is the threebanded courser, which tends to nest in the drier woodland areas.
ABOVE Although frequently spotted throughout the subcontinent, Botswana's pied kingfishers are restricted to its eastern parts.
RIGHT The blackwinged stilt is common near estuaries, marshes and pans.

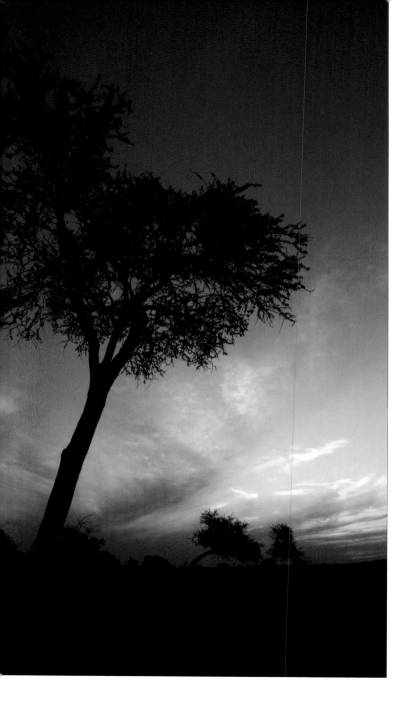

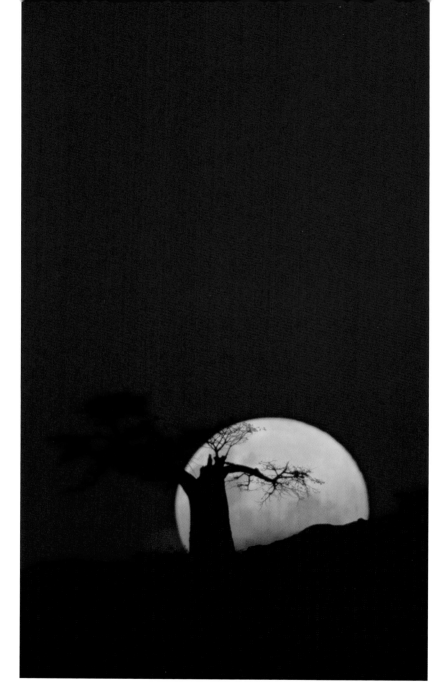

ABOVE, TOP RIGHT AND OPPOSITE Large sections of the drier parts of Botswana are virtually without trees, but in areas such as Tuli, where there is a good number, species include the shepherd's tree (above) and the baobab (top right and opposite).

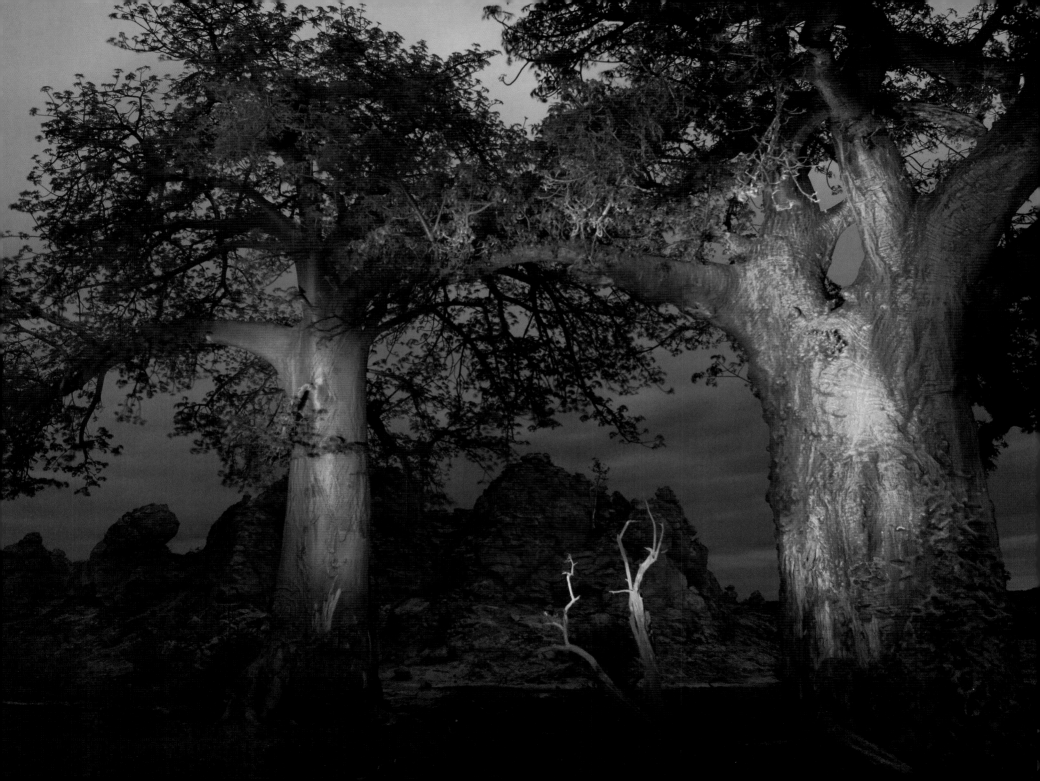

Zimbabwe

Of the about 390 000 square kilometres (150 000 square miles) that make up Zimbabwe, more than 6 million hectares (15 million acres) comprise terrain set aside as conservation land, which includes some of the most impressive wildlife populations in southern Africa. And, considering its vast untamed wildernesses and its even more breathtaking beauty, it is not surprising, then, that the country is one of the most acclaimed wildlife destinations on the continent.

While the latter years have seen a steady decline in the prosperity of both the country and its people and the political uncertainty that shrouds the nation continues to erode its true potential as one of southern Africa's gems, little can detract from the fact that Zimbabwe is indeed blessed with some of the subcontinent's most impressive landscapes. Although many of the urban settlements have yet to develop and grow to meet high international standards, Zimbabwe's natural wonders, its many attractions and the remarkable diversity of its wildlife and environs are still the country's most prominent

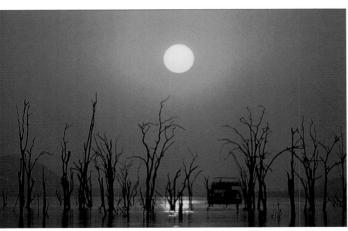

ABOVE *Set against a backdrop of magnificent hills, Lake Kariba is one of the continent's most impressive bodies of water.*

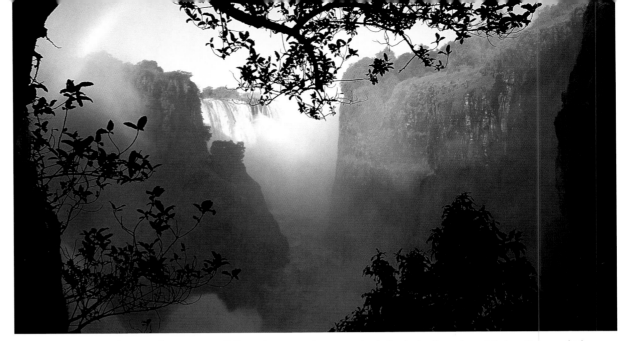

ABOVE *In Zimbabwe the magnificent Victoria Falls are known, quite appropriately by the local people, as Mosi-oa-Tunya, which means 'the smoke that thunders'.*

drawcards, and almost all its international visitors head straight for the country's national parks and games reserves.

Much treasured are not only cultural heritage sites, such as the ancient ruins of Great Zimbabwe, but also the many unique landmarks that have put Zimbabwe on the safari map. Prime among these must be the great 'smoke that thunders', the mighty roar of the Victoria Falls, tucked away in the northwestern corner of the country, bordering Zimbabwe's northern neighbour, Zambia. Situated on the waters of the majestic Zambezi – some 2 700 kilometres (1 678 miles) long – and alongside the national park that shares the river name, the massive waterfall at the centre of the Victoria Falls/Mosi-oa-Tunya World Heritage Site is a remarkable natural feature by any standard. The falls themselves are surrounded by a rugged rainforest and riverine environment and swathed in a heavy 'mist' that emanates from the impressive cascade that has captured the imagination of all those fortunate enough to have witnessed

its power. The falls and the rainforest that envelopes them are the focal point of the Victoria Falls National Park, some 2 300 hectares (5 680 acres) of riverine and woodland habitat bordering the impressive cascade. Lauded as one of the greatest natural phenomena in Africa, some 545 million litres (120 million gallons) of water plummet down Victoria Falls per minute when the Zambezi River is in flood, at its most impressive between the months of April and June and reaching its pinnacle at what are commonly known as the Main Falls.

The falls also form the very focal point of the travel industry in both Zimbabwe as well as Zambia. The Zambezi Gorge is, in fact, considered one of the greatest adventure spots in the world, not the least of which is for great white-water rafting. The Zambezi, at times gentle and slow and at others mercilessly violent in its charge towards the ocean, is dotted here and there with rapids. The Victoria Falls and the gorges that encircle them offer any number of further adventures, including bungee jumping down what appears to be bottomless pits of rock and water and spellbinding aerial flights over both the falls and the cliffs and valleys that surround them. Spread across this rugged landscape are plenty of opportunities for less-frenetic pursuits: a stroll through misty forests, hiking routes, 4x4 trails, big-game safaris and even a cruise down the snaking river. The immediate area surrounding the falls, acclaimed as the most spectacular landscape on the entire course of the Zambezi, is extraordinarily rich in the type of animal life typical of similar environs. Here, the traveller will encounter crocodiles and hippos, as well as elephant.

While considerably less developed than Victoria Falls National Park, which caters largely for the demands of the visiting public, the 56 000 hectares (138 350 acres) of the Zambezi National Park alone are home to lion, leopard, cheetah, elephant, rhino, buffalo and zebra, as well as a number of other species of the great Zambezi Basin.

The human history of Zimbabwe is, however, equally intriguing – if not even more so. While the nation boasts a wide sphere of cultural influences, from the Shona and

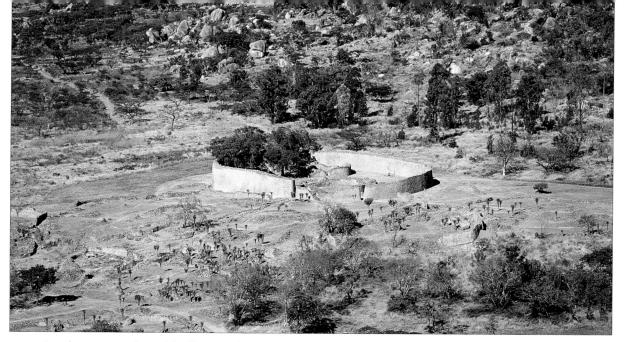

ABOVE In order to preserve the wealth of historic cultural heritage sites such as the ancient ruins of Great Zimbabwe, many have been incorporated into the nation's established parks and reserves.

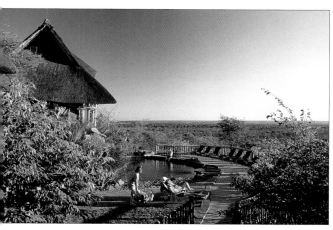

ABOVE A satellite industry has arisen around tourist facilities such as Victoria Falls Safari Lodge at Vic Falls.

Ndebele to people of Afro-Asian and European descent, it is, however, the people who once populated what is now commonly known as Great Zimbabwe who are the lingering legend of ancient Zimbabwe. While historical research is ongoing and provides a fascinating look at this remarkable conglomeration of great stone structures said to have been built some 700 years ago, it is known that the early occupants were prolific traders who bartered with gold extracted from the earth here and who kept large herds of cattle. Today, the most impressive man-made feature is the Great Enclosure, a massive, high-walled arena that may have been the private quarters of a royal dynasty that reigned over the region.

While many of the people of Zimbabwe are struggling to make ends meet and subsist from day to day on meagre earnings, worth less and less as the national economy declines, most continue to take exceptional pride in their status as Zimbabweans, many having fought long and hard for independence and freedom from colonial powers. Today,

many of Zimbabwe's citizens still eke out a living from the sought-after crafts for which they are justifiably renowned, most notably the stone carvings and basketware.

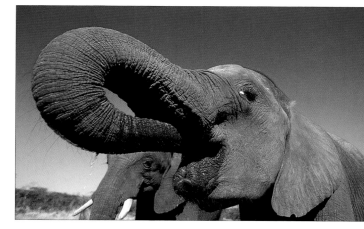

ABOVE The resident elephants at the Victoria Falls have given rise to the popular Elephant Camp.

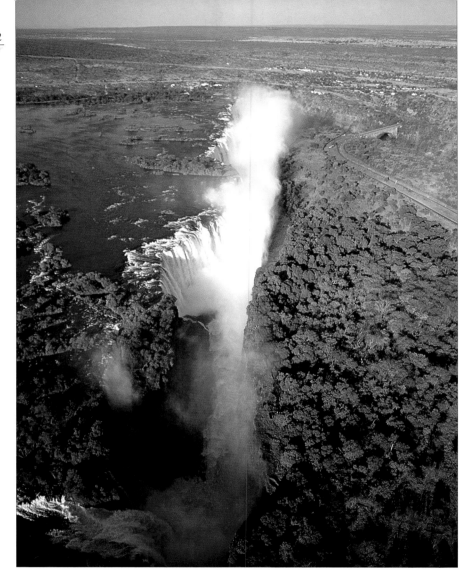

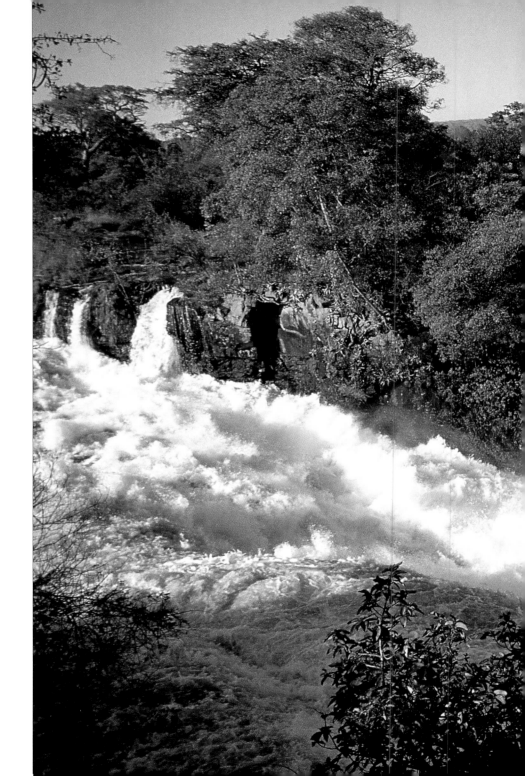

ABOVE AND RIGHT Situated on the Zambezi in a small rainforest that forms part of the national park, the dramatic Victoria Falls have long been lauded as one of the 'greatest spectacles on earth'. The waters crash some 100 metres (330 feet) down into the Zambezi Gorge, and the resulting spray – rising in parts about 500 metres (1 640 feet) into the air and covering sections of the surrounding forest – is said to be seen from miles around. The falls themselves, almost two kilometres (one mile) wide at their broadest point, actually fall within the political boundaries of both Zimbabwe and Zambia, and are skirted by a network of walks and trails that facilitate the best views for the many thousands of visitors who flock here annually.

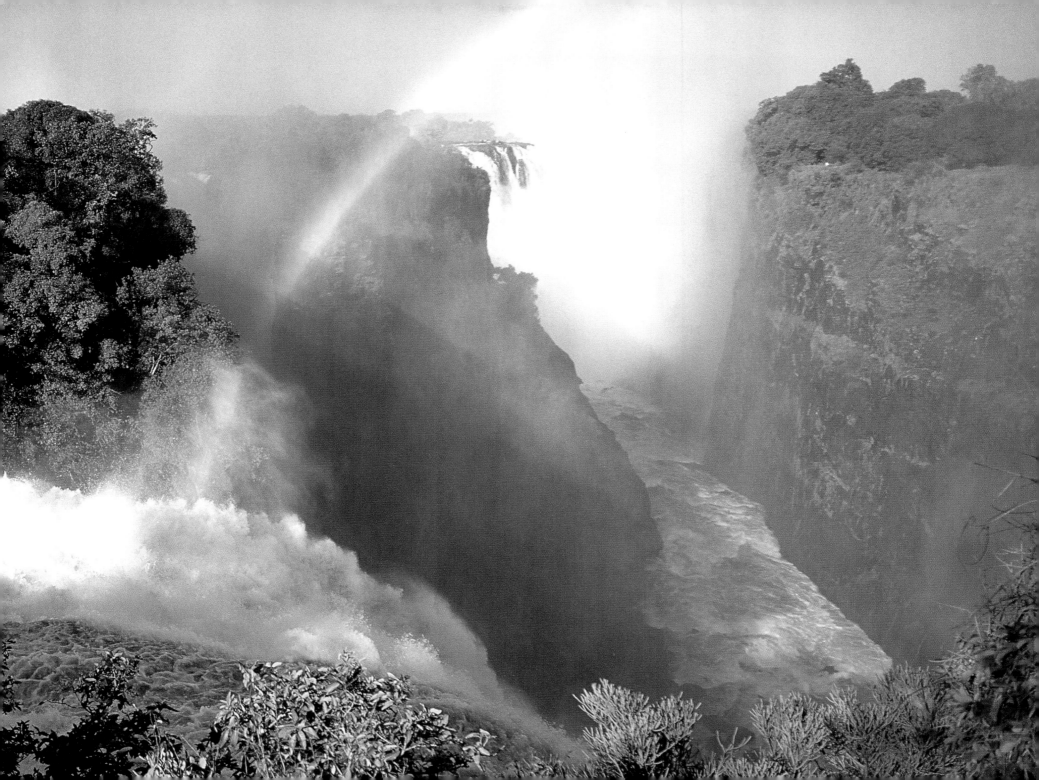

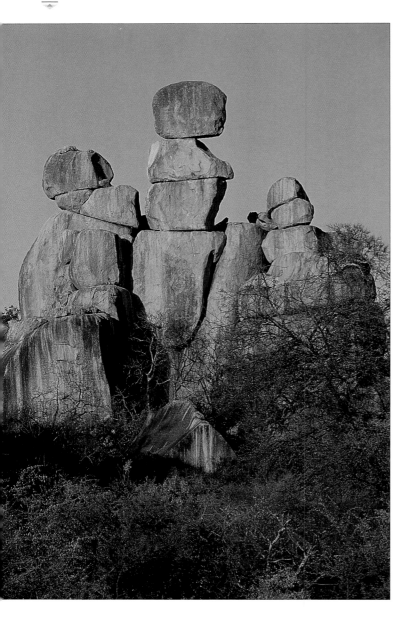

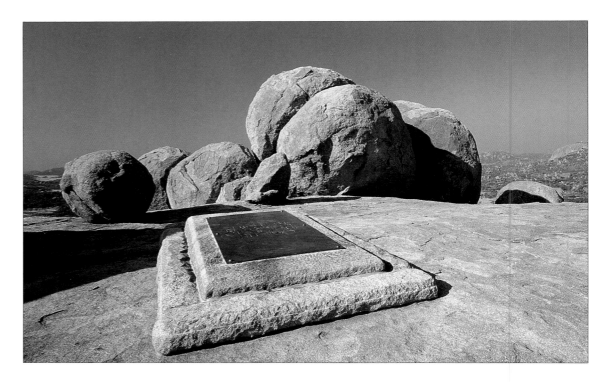

LEFT At the centre of the Matobo National Park, south of Bulawayo, is the unusual stone formation known as Mother and Child, a series of precariously balanced boulders and stones weathered by the corrosive combination of rain, wind and sand. Today, it is the rocky terrain of klipspringer, hyrax and lizards, and even the elusive leopard, as well as some of Africa's most recognisable birds of prey, including the black eagle.

ABOVE The rounded granite domes of Matobo are perhaps best known to Westerners as the site of the grave of statesman and industrialist Cecil John Rhodes, after whom Rhodesia – now known as Zimbabwe – was originally named by the colonial powers who administered the territory.

OPPOSITE The impressive stone-walled ruins of Great Zimbabwe is undoubtedly Africa's most impressive medieval site south of the Sahara, an archaeological and architectural masterpiece said to be more than 700 years old. The imposing settlement was established by ancestors of the Shona people known as the Karonga, and consists of a series of walls that were once schools and markets, grain stores and places of worship.

OVERLEAF The harsh African sun sets over Lake Kariba in Zimbabwe's Matusadona National Park.

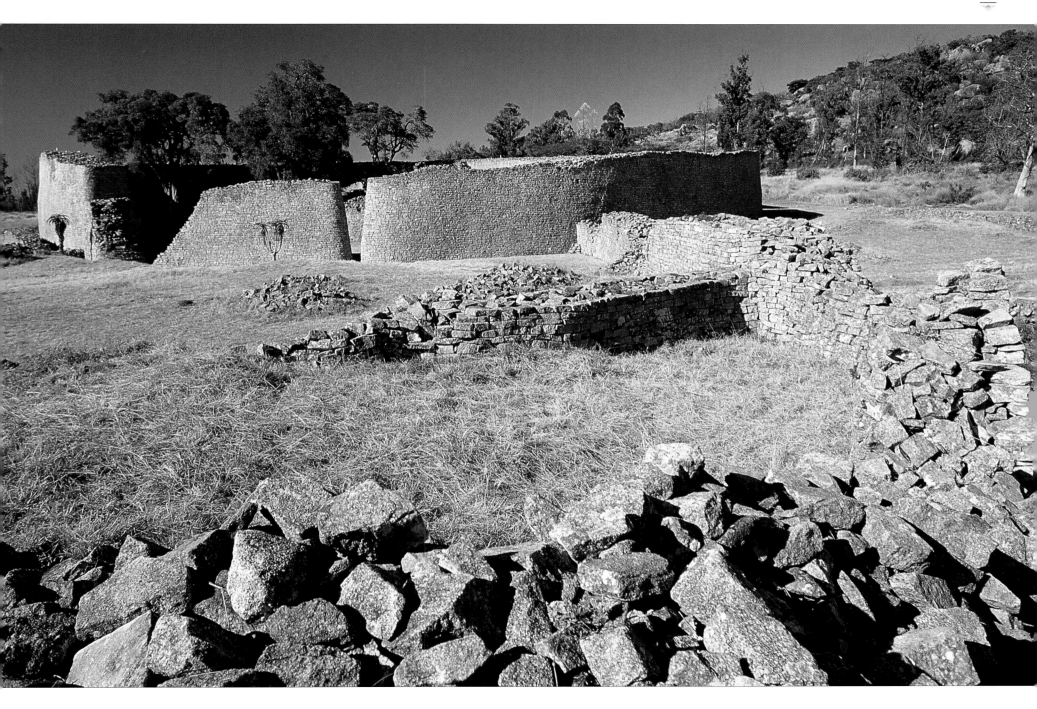

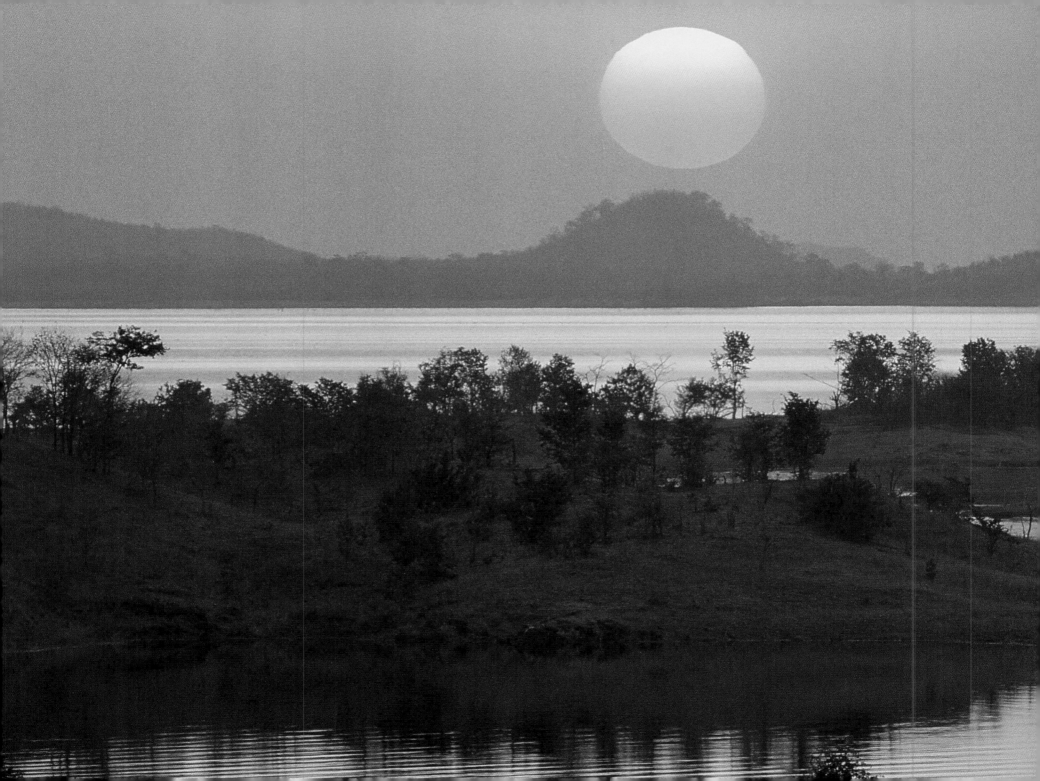

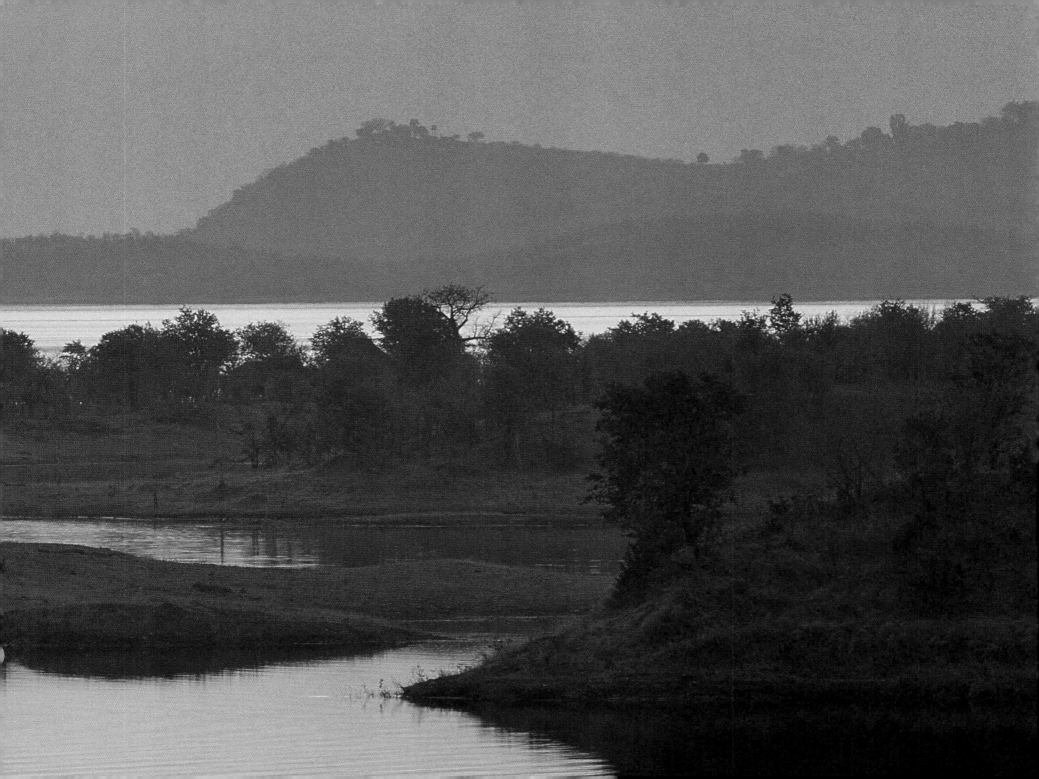

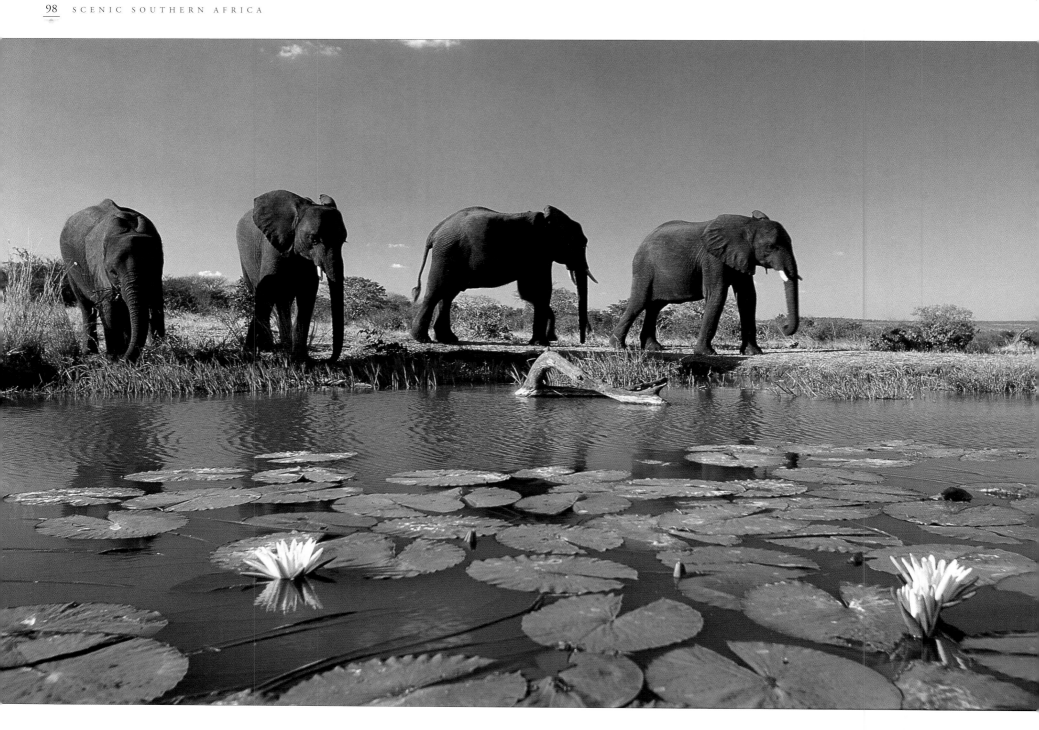

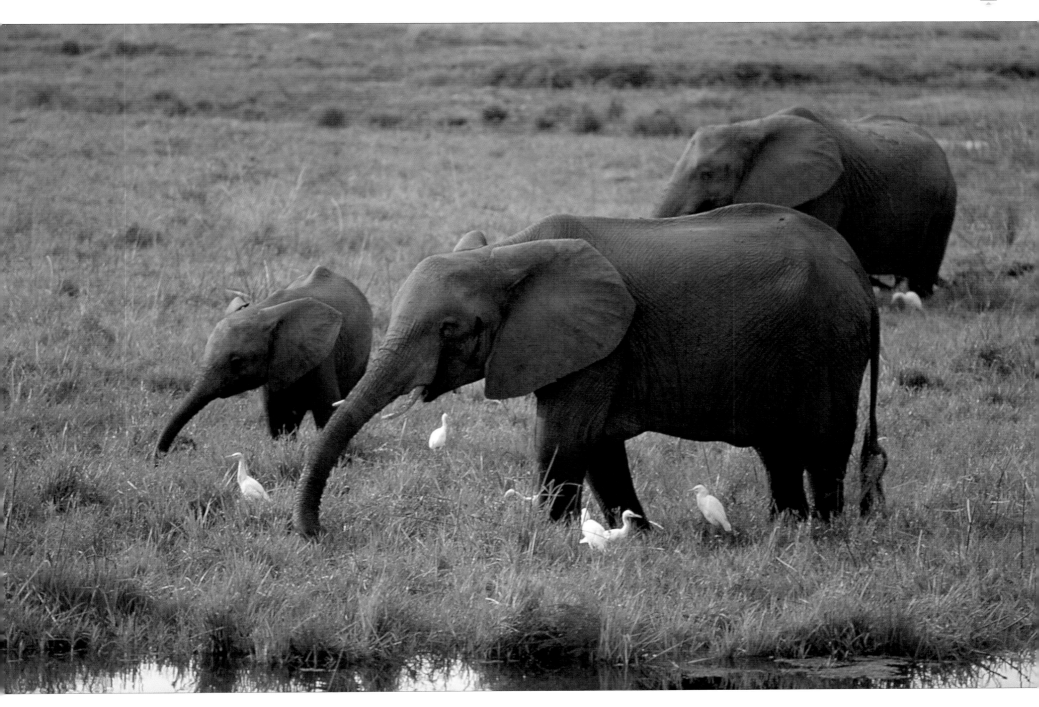

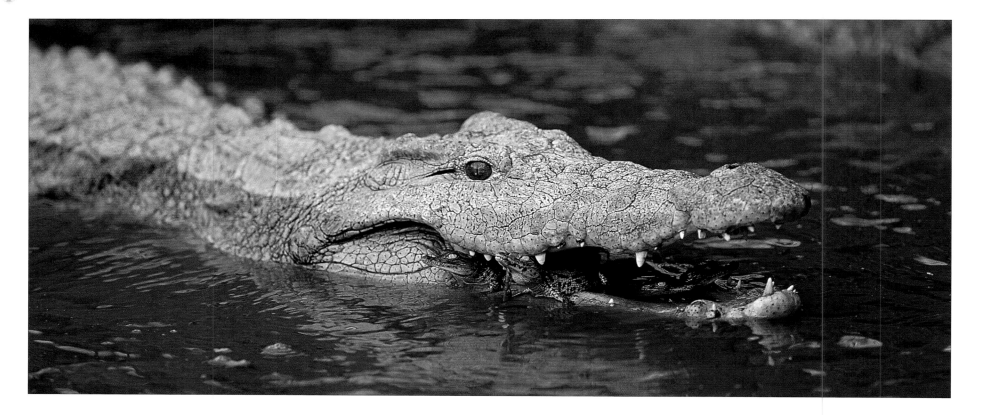

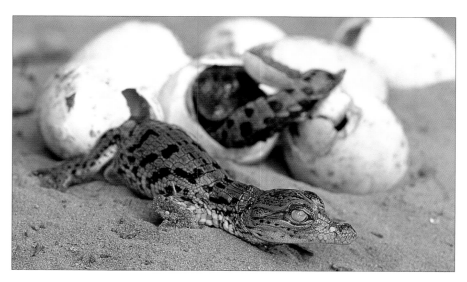

PREVIOUS PAGES, LEFT AND RIGHT Game-watching in Zimbabwe, particularly in its top parks –
Gonarezhou, Chimanimani, Hwange, Mana Pools, Matobo, Nyanga and Matusadona – is
an extremely rewarding experience. The most prominent national parks offer good sightings
of buffalo, crocodile and other big mammals, such as the African elephant. For the latter
especially, visitors should stop over at Mana Pools, a World Heritage Site.

ABOVE AND LEFT Of all the creatures in and around the Zambezi, it is the Nile crocodile that
lurks in its murky waters that represents – in the popular imagination, anyway – the greatest
danger. These reptiles with an ancient genetic record reach a length of about three metres.
Crocodiles generally lay 20 to 80 eggs at a time and the hatchlings make their appearance
after a three-month incubation. Prior to hatching, the youngsters emit a high-pitched noise
that warns the mother that it is time to uncover the nest.

OPPOSITE Sable antelope, with their contrasting hide patterns and scimitar-like horns, occur
virtually throughout Zimbabwe, especially areas that offer open woodland or grasslands.
Herds tend to be divided into the territorial male, nursing female and bachelors.

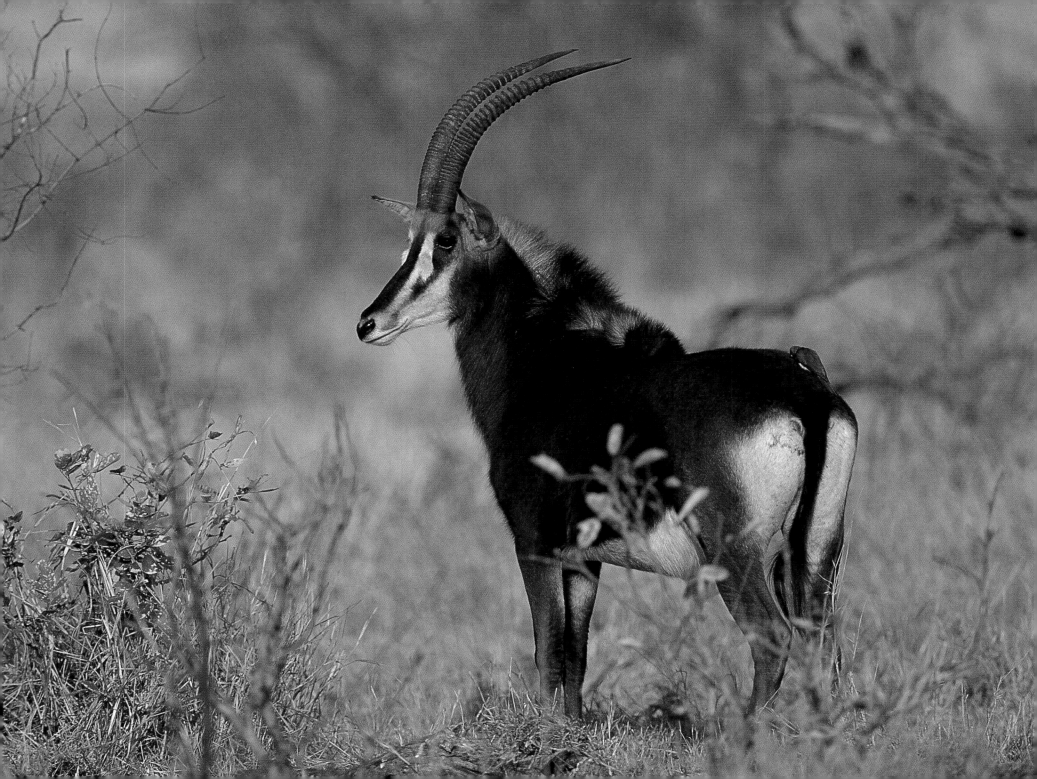

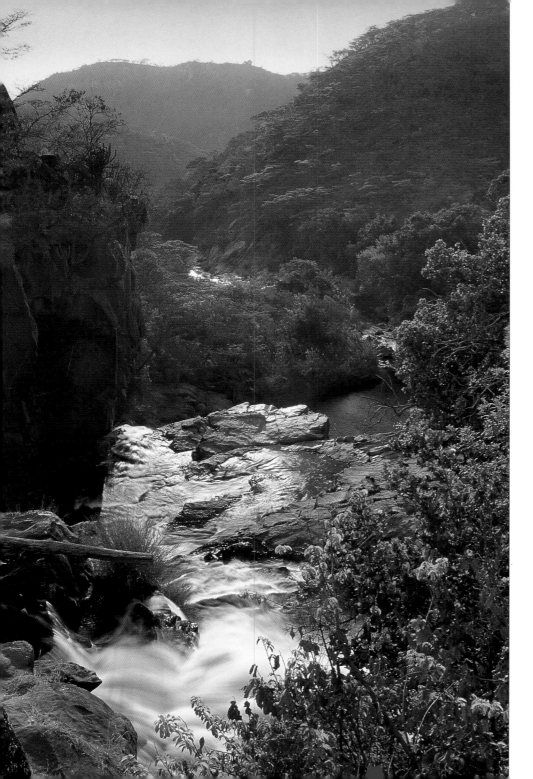

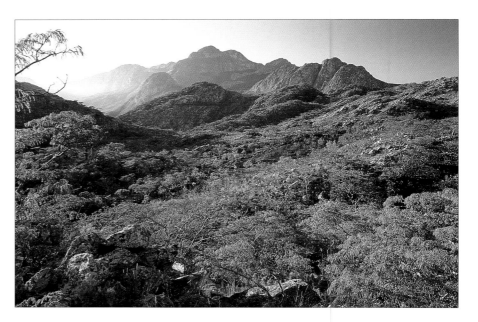

LEFT Although no match for the mighty waterfalls of the Zambezi Gorge, the impressive cascade of the Nyangombe Falls makes for one of the area's most exciting and rewarding walking and hiking trails.

ABOVE The massive granite mountains of the Chimanimani range – which, in fact, extends into Mozambique – are peaked by the summits of Kweza and Mawenje looming over the Chimanimani National Park that lies spread across its slopes. Although relatively small compared to other parks in Zimbabwe, it is generally considered one of its most unspoilt, many parts virtually impassable except on foot. Today, much of the territory is crisscrossed with a series of paths and trails that cover much of the mountainous terrain, despite its apparent inaccessibility. Conquering the rugged landscape on foot, however, is not without its rewards – the expansive views from the upper slopes are, almost without exception, unmatched. Towards the lower end of the valley stand the forest reserves of Haroni and Rusitu, Zimbabwe's only lowland rainforests, themselves home to an extraordinary variety of forest flora and fauna.

OPPOSITE Gonarezhou National Park is hot and very dry, characterised by steep sandstone cliffs and vast plains repopulated as recently as the 1960s with the wildlife that was once found naturally in the region. Today, Gonarezhou – which means 'place of the elephant' – forms part of the all-encompassing Gaza-Kruger-Gonarezhou Transfrontier Park, which incorporates South Africa's Kruger and Mozambique's Banhine reserve. As such, its wildlife populations, including the lion that roam the Chilojo Hills, enjoy far greater protection than ever before.

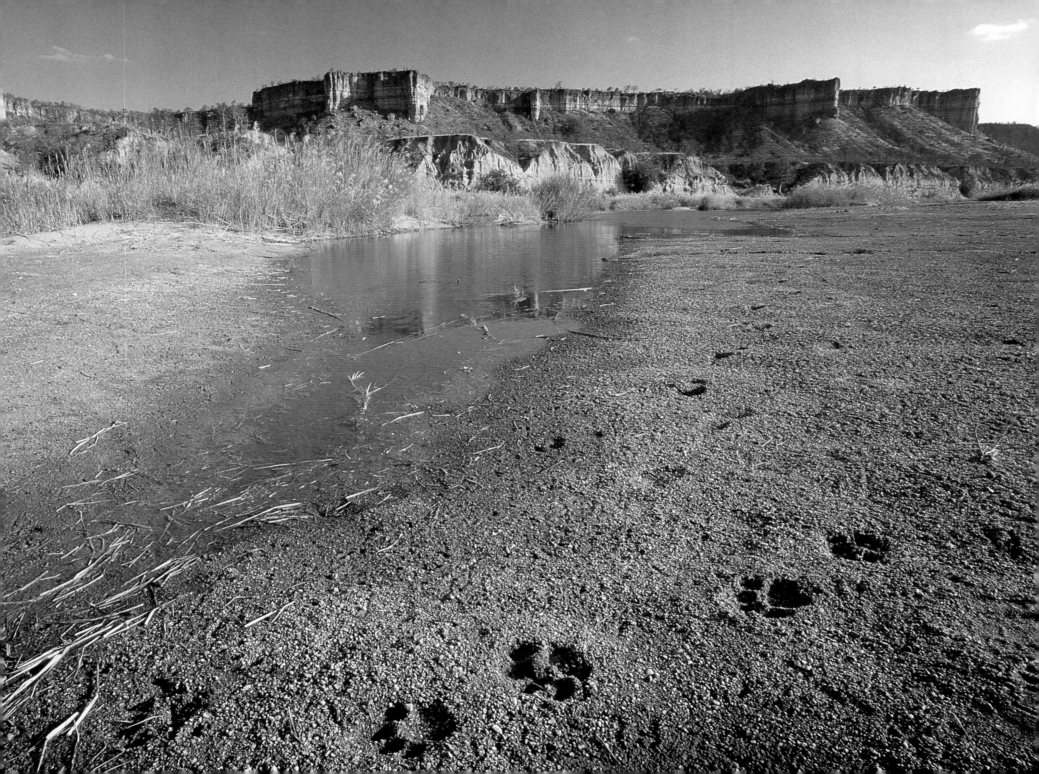

Mozambique

Mozambique is covered for the most part by what appears to be boundless savanna fringed by forested highlands and a lush coast of lagoons and coral reefs that continue to attract travellers and adventurers. Its people are friendly and open, and endlessly hospitable. Visitors to this part of southern Africa are inevitably met with a laugh and a smile, and while poverty has left its unmistakable mark, most especially on the remote villages, the sense of pride and human dignity that pervades much of Mozambique remains its enduring quality.

It is, however, the extraordinary landscape and, more importantly, its fine coastline that makes Mozambique one of Africa's premier holiday destinations – but this does little to detract from the scenic beauty of the interior. Inland Mozambique is as enthralling as its picture-postcard coastal fringe. The province of Maputo in the southern stretch of the

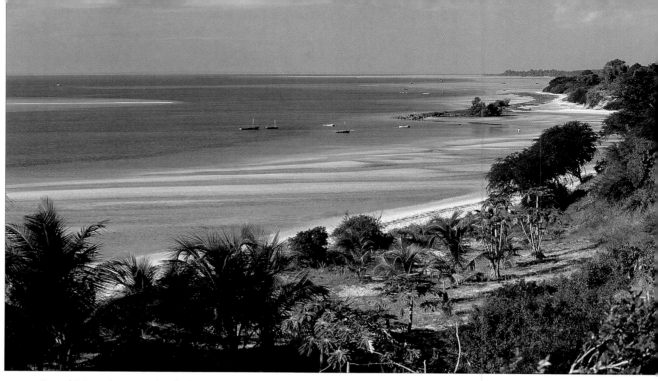

ABOVE Coastal Mozambique is a beach idyll, the Caribbean of Africa. The scenic splendour stretches from rows of picture-postcard palm trees, across soft sands to a gentle, blue sea and beyond.

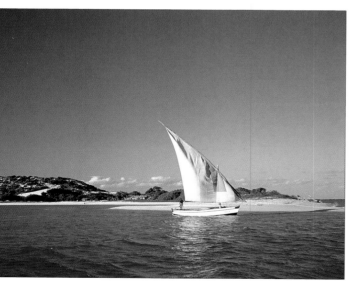

ABOVE The dhows that ply the waters off Magaruque are typical of those that cruise virtually the entire Mozambique coast.

country is the most developed and boasts just about everything travellers may expect in Africa: historic old villages, breathtaking vistas and mile after endless mile of winding road weaving across the heart of the country. It is thus a perfect combination of all that is popularly considered 'truly African'.

Mozambique's political boundaries enclose some 800 000 square kilometres (310 000 square miles), divided into 10 provinces of which Maputo, Inhambane, Zambezia and Nampula are the most significant from a tourism standpoint. Because so many of its people still make up tight-knit rural communities, the country's cultural heritage remains an integral part of even modern society and its indigenous customs and traditions are practised with enthusiasm by the majority of Mozambique's approximately 17 million citizens. About half of the population is of the Makua-Lomwe group

and about a quarter Tsonga, with some 60 per cent following traditional beliefs. With a remarkably varied social mix, it is of little surprise, then, that the city of Maputo – in the southernmost corner of the province of the same name – is one of southern Africa's most vibrant capitals. Known until quite recently as Lourenço Marques – a remnant of the Portuguese colonial heritage – the capital started out as little more than a small rural community but, over some 400 years, has grown into an energetic port city. It has been more than a decade since the country saw the cessation of hostilities in the civil strife that gripped the nation for a number of years, and Maputo is slowly being rebuilt. While a number of its grand old buildings – its colonial palaces, mosques and museums, for example – still carry the scars of those war-torn years, the latter-day city is becoming more and more cosmopolitan. Maputo plays proud host to an increasing island chain that makes up the famed Bazaruto Archipelago. The island group consists of four main islands – Bazaruto, Magaruque, Benguerra, and St Carolina (known, unsurprisingly, as Paradise Island to many visitors) – as well as smaller islets rimmed with a prolific and vibrantly hued reef system that, together, make up the archipelago, which is now a national park. Lashed by wind and the strong currents of the ocean and its waves, this marine environment is well protected by the nation's relatively rigid conservation guidelines. The warm waters – courtesy of the Benguela Current that flows southward from the equator – are crystal clear, which makes viewing the spectacular underwater world as easy as if you were seeing it through the lens of a camera. The marine life here is both colourful and astonishingly diverse: brilliant hard and stony corals, tiny fish flitting among the rocks and crevices beneath the surface of the water, anemones and other invertebrate species, as well as turtles. Diving is thus an unparalleled experience, providing unique opportunities to explore some of the most remarkable seascapes of southern Africa.

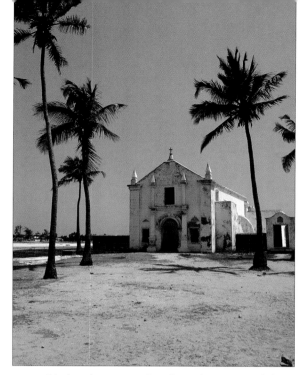

ABOVE Much architecture, such as the 18th-century Catholic cathedral on Mozambique Island, remains colonial in style.

number of international travellers intent on catching a glimpse of Africa that, in most other places on the continent, is lost forever.

The sky-blue ocean and palm-fringed, sandy beaches that skirt approximately 1 000 kilometres (620 miles) of the curve that is the Mozambican shore – stretching between Maputo in the south and Beira in the north – comprise some of the country's most significant natural habitats. This stretch of coastline is home to southern Africa's only population of the whale-like dugong, which is threatened with extinction, and an abundance of spectacular coral reefs. Here, too, are opportunities for recreational fishing of every kind, from big-game to angling, but of course there are also excellent opportunities for diving. The Mozambican coast is high on the list of top international diving locations, most notably the some 20 kilometres (12 miles) around the picturesque

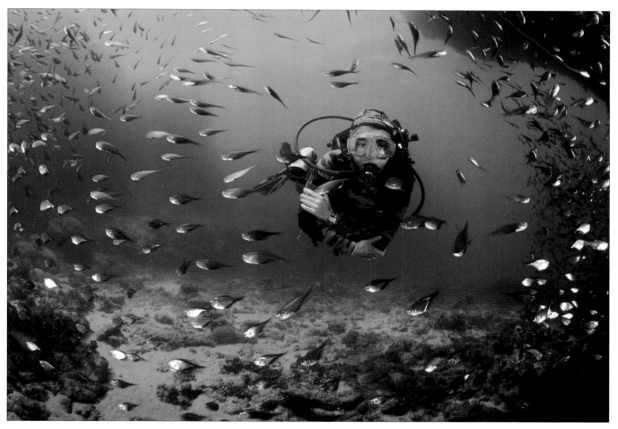

ABOVE The cave at the entrance to the 'Pemba playground' – a veritable underwater wonderland that offers treasures for divers who flock to these breathtaking reefs – shimmers with the abundance of glassies.

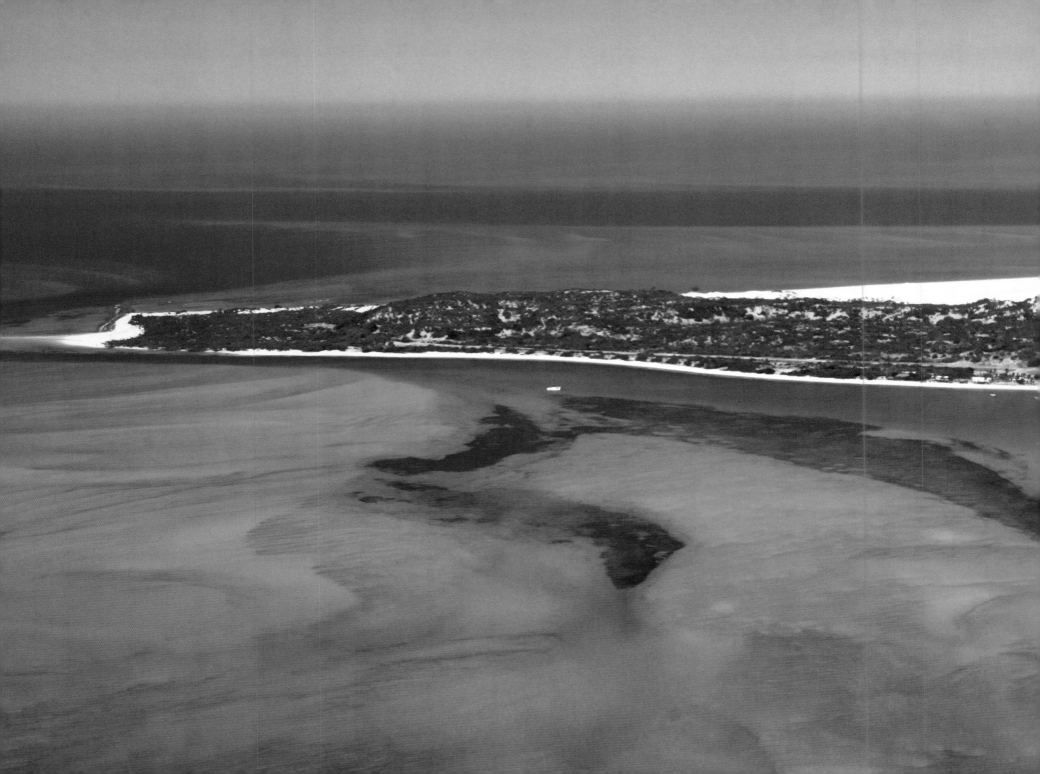

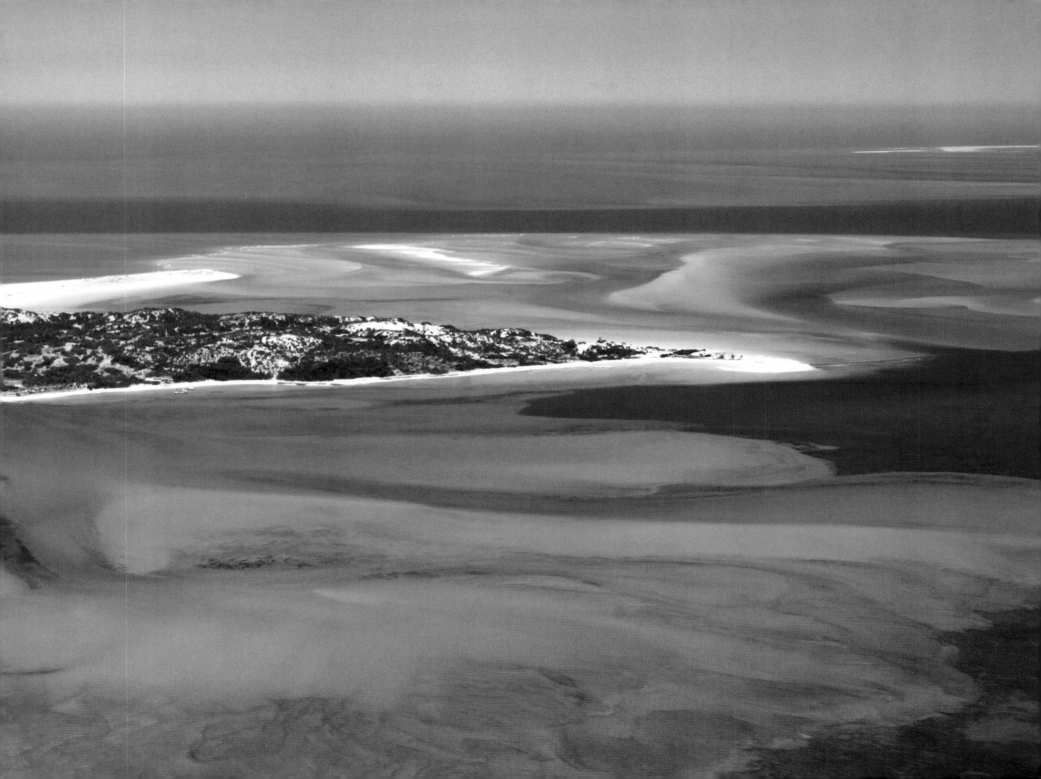

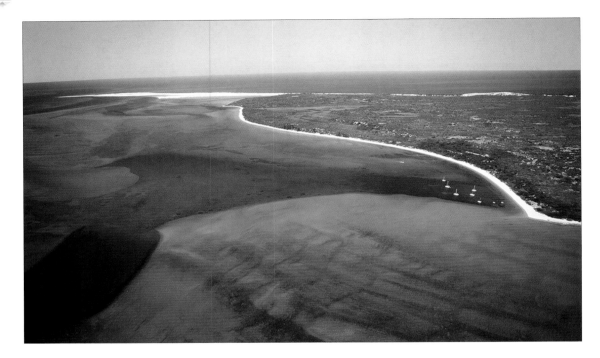

PREVIOUS PAGES Magaruque Island, which is known locally as Ilha de Magaruque, lies within the legendary Bazaruto Archipelago, its entire circumference comprising one empty but dazzling beach after another. A handful of similarly pristine stretches of sand along Mozambique's coastline have been developed into up-market resorts that cater almost exclusively for a foreign clientele in search of a beach paradise.

OPPOSITE With an extensive coastline that extends from the cold waters of the Atlantic on southern Africa's western seaboard right round to the warm Indian Ocean on the east, the subcontinent boasts many tranquil, unspoilt beaches but it is those of Mozambique, specifically that at Vilanculos, that remain some of the most picturesque. Conservation and tourism initiatives help protect many of these scenically splendid coastal areas.

ABOVE Vilanculos is one of Mozambique's principal mainland towns and, as such, is served not only by an airport, but also one of the most scenic harbours in southern Africa.

RIGHT With the development of southern Africa's tourism potential, initiatives such as the plush Benguerra Lodge are rapidly becoming popular drawcards to visitors.

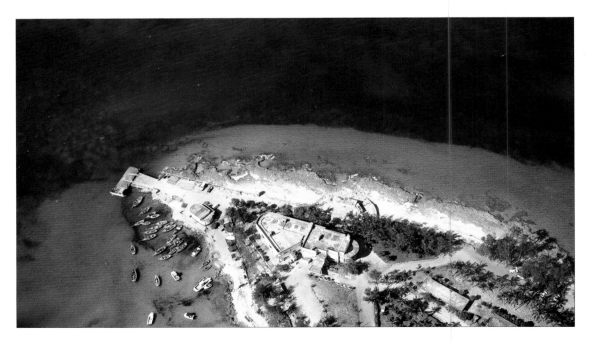

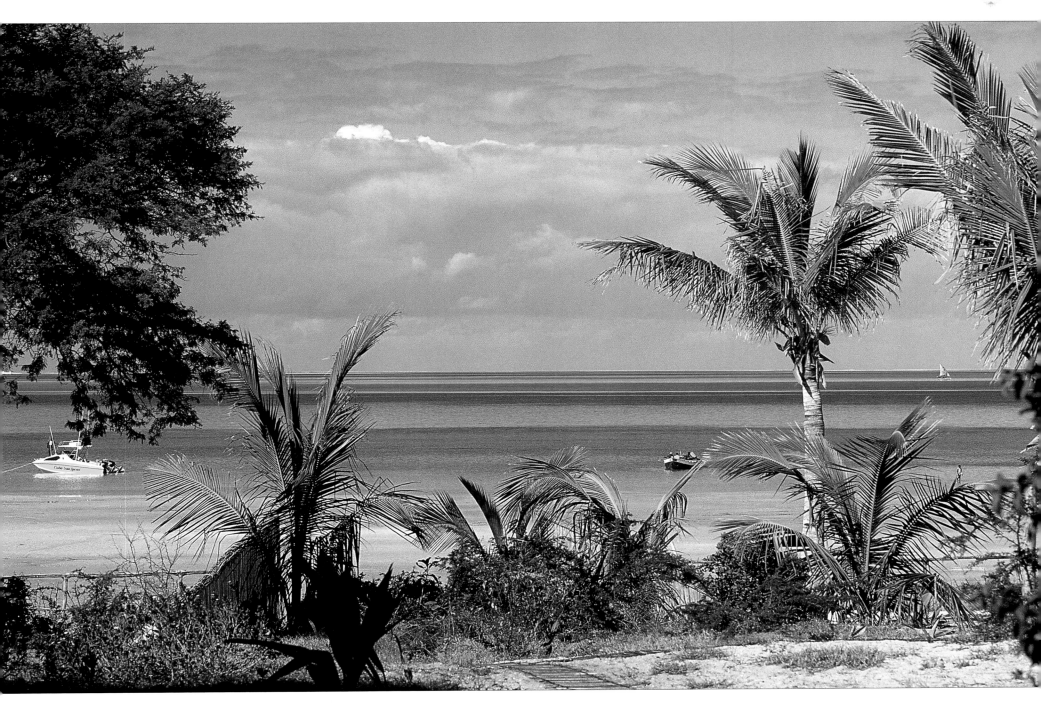

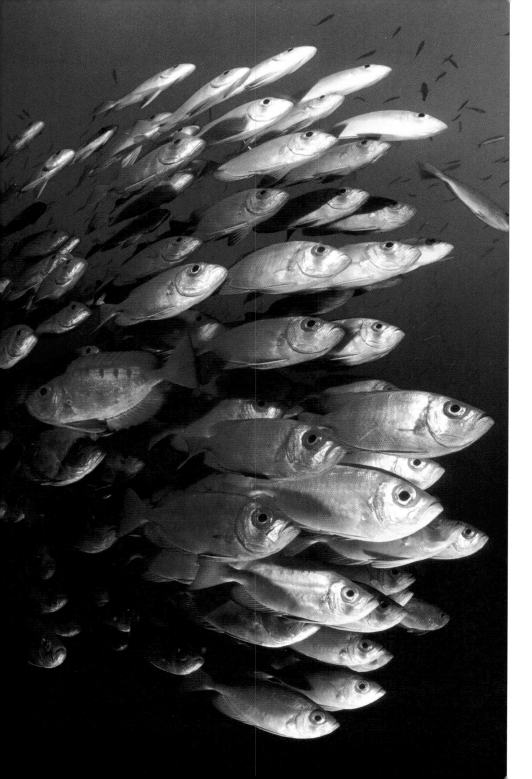

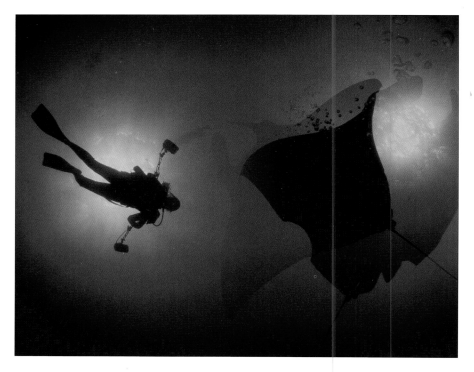

LEFT AND OPPOSITE Blue waters and white, sandy beaches lined with palms and edged with coral reefs stretch for about 1 000 kilometres (620 miles) along the coast of Mozambique. It is, therefore, little wonder that it is one of the premier diving destinations on the subcontinent, boasting as it does some of the most remarkable reefs in the western Indian Ocean. Not only is this marine habitat a long-established tourist spot, but it is also a popular destination for coastal and big-game fishing, attracting anglers, snorkellers and deep-sea fishermen.

ABOVE The Mozambique Channel is a unique marine environment, its nature dictated by sea levels, currents and wind direction and its waters crystal clear, splashed at regular intervals with the luminescent colours of its diverse sea life – the bright colours of its anemones and corals, huge shoals of fish, green turtles and such impressive sea creatures as manta rays. Naturally, the water clarity and wealth of marine life on view are virtually unparalleled, offering some of the most rewarding underwater experiences in southern Africa.

OVERLEAF Because of its long, impressive coastline, opportunities to explore beach and sea abound in Mozambique, and the little seaside town of Vilanculos (pictured), for example, provides easy access to some of the most scenic and protected waters in southern Africa, as well as the splendour of the Bazaruto Archipelago. It is well developed for travellers, and on its doorstep is a string of beaches, as well as of opportunities to go birding, fishing and diving.

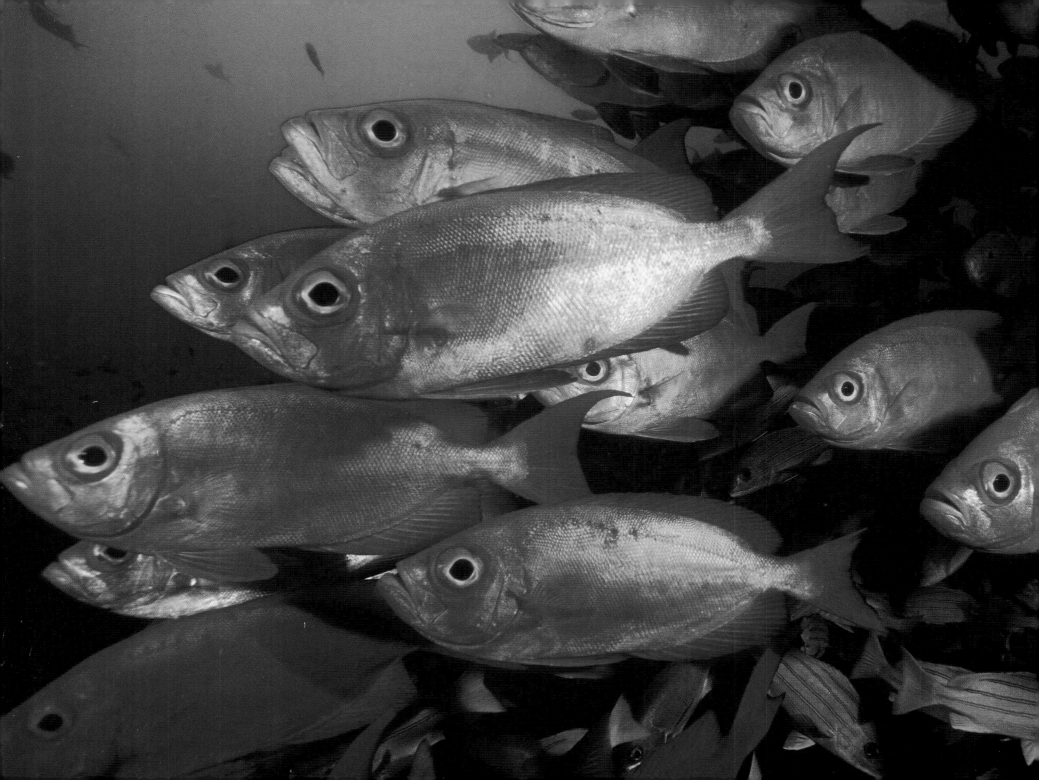

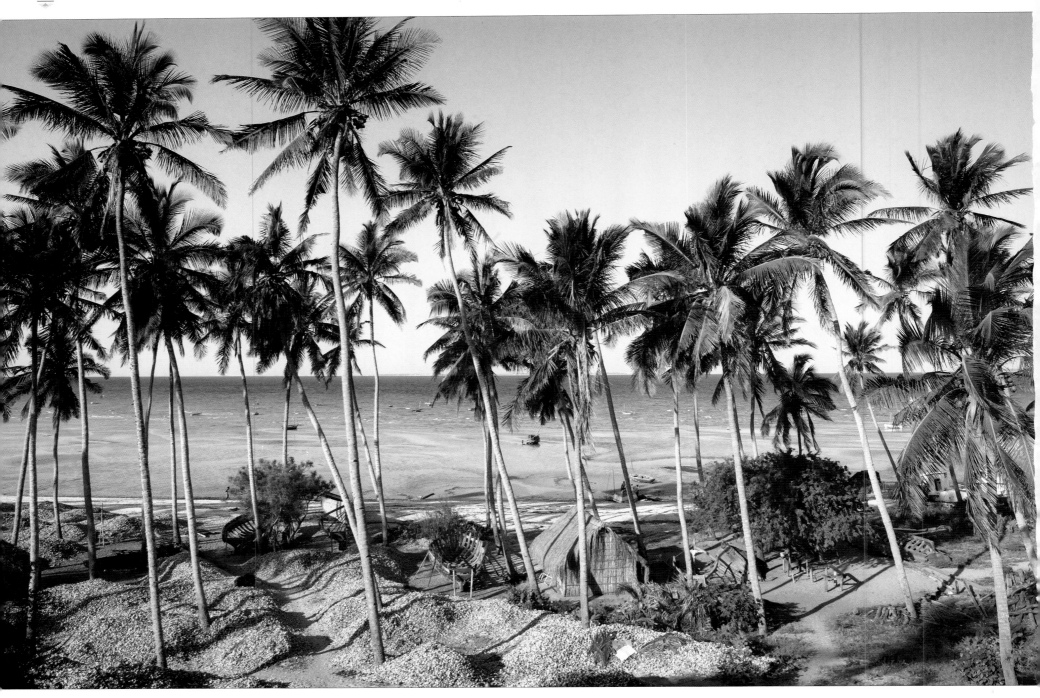